Guided by the Spirits

Guided by the Spirits is a case study of youth suicide in the Sault Sainte Marie Tribe of Chippewa Indians. Written by a member of the tribal community, this study focuses on qualitative methods, indigenous experience, and collaborative approaches to explore the social and historical significance of youth suicide in an Ojibwa community. *Guided by the Spirits* combines traditional methods of analysis, extracts of interviews and field notes, and creative ethnographic writing to present the relationships between culture, history, identity, agency, and youth suicide. This book is a must read for lay readers, policy makers, and researchers who seek a window into contemporary Native American life as well as a critical interpretation of youth suicide in indigenous societies.

Seth Allard, MA, is a cultural anthropologist, Pipe Carrier and Ogichiidaa of the Bowheting Ojibwa, and a member of the Sault Sainte Marie Tribe of Chippewa Indians. He has a master's degree in anthropology from Western Michigan University, and his research focuses on indigenous culture and history and medical anthropology.

Guided by the Spirits

The Meanings of Life, Death, and Youth Suicide in an Ojibwa Community

Seth Allard

Routledge
Taylor & Francis Group
LONDON AND NEW YORK

First published 2018 by Routledge

2 Park Square, Milton Park, Abingdon, Oxfordshire OX14 4RN
52 Vanderbilt Avenue, New York, NY 10017

Routledge is an imprint of the Taylor & Francis Group, an informa business

First issued in paperback 2019

Library of Congress Cataloging-in-Publication Data
A catalog record for this book has been requested

ISBN: 978-0-8153-6944-8 (hbk)
ISBN: 978-0-367-25738-5 (pbk)

Typeset in Sabon
by Apex CoVantage, LLC

This work is dedicated to

Our children, grandchildren and the future generations of Anishnaabek. You are amongst the seventh generation, which my generation was brought into this world to serve. Yours will be a time of peace, prosperity and joy. This work is one of many steps toward that end by those who are devoted to you and to your future.

The families who experienced the many pains associated with youth suicide. I hope that this work will provide healing, a sense of understanding and reconciliation.

The elders and teachers of ceremony and language. For so long you have been a bulwark against a would-be fading away of our people. Our status in the overall history of humanity is rising from an oft-overlooked footnote to an inspiring feature of human strength and resilience. Any successes that we enjoy are a direct result of your efforts, your often quiet, every day, moral enactments of Anishnaabek identity.

The young men and women who feel hopeless and unloved. You are loved by many people and Kitchi Manitou. There is always hope for a better tomorrow and a fulfilling life—even if the world around you seems to tell you otherwise.

The youth who have walked on from this world as a result of suicide. You were made to believe that you lived in a world that you did not belong to, did not accept you or love you. Many Anishnaabek and community members feel that you passed from a physical world that held pain and torment to a spiritual world of peace and joy. Of the many beliefs that I have adopted from the community, I hold this one closest to my heart.

Finally, to my beautiful son Liam, who believes that a monster can be turned into a good person with a simple hug. He teaches me that understanding, embracing and forgiving the ugliest aspects of our history, society and even ourselves brings about an enjoyable and healthy life. If only the world knew, huh, Lilo?

I now find myself embarking on a story that I do not feel worthy or able to tell. I say Bozhoo, Bozhoo . . . it is now time to speak. I ask you to pray that my words have power and meaning—that my voice is Guided by the Spirits.

Contents

Figures

Maps

Preface

Bozhoo, Bozhoo,
Anii, Mueshka Miikan Bemosed Indizhnikaaz, Mukwa Dodaim, Bowheting Indoonjibaa.
(Greetings, my name is Man Who Walks the Red Road, I am of the Bear Clan, and my Ancestral Home is Bowheting, a place now known as Sault Sainte Marie, Michigan).

My three-and-a-half-year-old son jumps up on my lap as I write, scrunches his face and asks "What are you doing?" I look back into his almond eyes and give him what I think is the best answer. "I am telling a story," I say. As it turns out, that is the best description for what I am attempting to do as I write about my recent fieldwork experience studying youth suicide in the Sault Sainte Marie Tribe of Chippewa Indians. Looking up from the computer screen and out the window at the thin blanket of snow that this year's mild winter has brought, I think on how the Ojibwa told stories in the lodge as a way to entertain and educate themselves in these harsher months. Over time, winter became the season of stories.

Stories are special things, whether one is telling or listening. Stories are not only our human attempt at making sense of the world around us, but serve as a guide for how we should feel and behave. Therefore, the power of stories exists in everything that we do. We hear, see, and ultimately enact the stories handed down to us in our roles as individuals fulfilling a role given by family and friends, as well as the more interconnected roles we play in schools, police departments, hospitals, religious and spiritual organizations, government, and other social institutions that operate in our community.

A powerful story is made up of three parts: Question, Answer, and Purpose. When these three parts come together, we can gain an understanding of our past, present, and future that is powerful and life altering. The confusion and pain that takes root in our lives can also be replaced by enlightenment and joy. Without any of these three parts, a story will remain hidden, and so too will the joy that is there for us.

What most effectively prevents a good, healing story from being told, listened to, and believed in is our sense of fear and desire—the fear that we will be exposed to the areas of our past or present that we do not wish to acknowledge, and the desire we often have to pursue a false sense of identity or what we see as a desirable lifestyle. Fear can push us away from personal discovery, while desire pulls us toward enticing and in the end harmful rewards. Together, these forces can paralyze individuals, families, and whole communities. Depending on the story, individuals, families, and communities can see a future that is hopeful, or one that is hopeless.

The Ojibwa are quite used to stories. The Ojibwa pass on oral history and traditions, or the memories and teachings handed down from person to person and generation to generation, through stories—with each story weaving into other stories. We express stories through Anishnaabemowin, the language of the Anishnaabek, with each word grounded in our history and the holistic way we see the world. The tapestry of our history, however damaged, is still one of beauty sewn into us from birth, with each generation adding its own weaves and patterns. It would only make sense, then, that when I heard from Tribal members and elders through everyday conversation that youth suicide was an issue in our community, I would immediately think on it, and eventually try to explain youth suicide as a story.

It is our tradition, however, that before telling a story, speaking in front of others, praying, or committing ourselves to an important undertaking, we acknowledge the people, events, and spirits that have inspired us to speech or action. For that reason the preface, acknowledgements, and dedications are the first sections written. Whether the moment includes thousands of people at one time or a thousand moments between only a few, the first act is to acknowledge what it is that brought us to each significant moment.

The Ojibwa continue to practice the tradition of saying Bozhoo before speaking in public and at spiritual gatherings. I have heard that Bozhoo may originate from the French greeting, Bonjour. While the French were the first European explorers to the Upper Great Lakes area, and to this day, many Ojibwa have strong French ancestry, Bozhoo is not to be confused with Bonjour. Some Ojibwa use Bozhoo as a loose greeting, without a thorough knowledge of why exactly it is that we say Bozhoo.

Bozhoo is a word that when uttered reminds us of our spiritual traditions and is said as a short prayer to our Creator before an important moment. The word is rooted in the last half of Nanabozhoo, the name of the central figure of many Ojibwa oral histories. By saying Bozhoo, we remember that, like Nanabozhoo, we are creatures of both spirit and body and as such, we can be wise, foolish, courageous, and fearful. Bozhoo is a way of saying—help me—help me speak well. If I falter or am anxious, it is only because this is important to my people and me. By saying Bozhoo, we also remember those spiritual forces that surround us—

Ki-Chi-Manitou, the Great Spirit

The Four Directions—Wabenong (East), Jawanong (South), Epighizhmuk (West) and Kewadinong (North)—and all that those four directions represent

Akii Manitou, the Spirit of the Earth
Ishpeming, the Spirit of the Sky
And finally, our own Spirits.

Acknowledgments

This series is a work of many hands. Family, Elders, community members and leaders, teachers within the Ojibwa traditional medicine community and social science circles, sacred places, Spirits of those who walked on, and family and friends have all aided and inspired the journey that this project has become. This short monograph, and the future work that stems from it, could not be complete without the community members who participated in formal interviews and open, emotional, and frank discussions. You shared and trusted me with your thoughts and stories. To you all I say Chi Miigwech.

To the American Philosophical Society Phillips Fund for providing a grant in support of early stages of research. For decades, the Phillips Fund has provided support for cultural and linguistic research in Native American communities. Chi Miigwech.

Bilinda, Sarah, Joe, and most recently Michael, you helped and challenged me, forming me into the scholar that I am (or one day will become). As a result, your words, examples as scholars, and passion for studying human history and culture are inherently present in this work. That being said, if you did not like the work, then perhaps I should have had different teachers! However, I believe that the knowledge, skills, and direction you provided were uniquely and powerfully suited to the completion of this work, and I will always be grateful to have you as my teachers and colleagues.

Thank you to the editors from Taylor and Francis, especially Nina Guttapalle. Turning an overly ambitious master's thesis into a book seemed a bit of a dream, yet you saw the importance of this work and made it a reality. Chi Miigwech.

I am indebted to many individuals in the Tribal community, including, but not limited to, Brother John Hascall, Mick Freshette, Lesly Ruditus, Henry Boulley, Les Ailing, Cecil Pavlat, Leonard Kimewon, and countless others. You gave spiritual teachings, friendship, and commonsense advice, questioned, challenged, and shaped the focus and meaning of this work—and in the process, made the work and the researcher better than either could hope to be. Chi Miigwech.

Description of Indigenous Peoples

The literature on youth suicide, as well as other areas of study, including the indigenous peoples residing in the United States and Canada, include many terms and acronyms describing this general population: AI/AN (American Indian/Alaska Native), 'Canadian First Nation,' 'American Indian,' 'Indian,' and 'Native American.' Application of general terms and acronyms, however, ignores the many cultural, linguistic, political, geographical, and socioeconomic differences between the hundreds of indigenous groups historically residing in the United States and Canada. Each indigenous group, historically referred to by the Western world as Tribes or bands—terms eventually adopted, at least in certain contexts, by indigenous communities themselves—is ascribed a title that delineates an ethnic group and subgroup (Tribe and Band-Clan), and is culturally and historically significant. Failing to use specific titles effectively casts aside the histories of indigenous communities and perpetuates a falsely concrete sense of Pan-Indianism. In order to avoid this error in description, the specific ethnic names and titles of indigenous groups are included as primary descriptors when referring to the community involved in this study and when referencing sources on indigenous youth suicide and behavioral health studies. For instance, when referring to a study of the White Mountain Apache (Barlow et al., 2012), "White Mountain Apache" will be directly inserted in a description of the work cited in order to avoid lumping "White Mountain Apache" history and culture into a Pan-Indian identity.

Use of the terms Native American and Canadian First Nation also represents a failure to recognize the geo-political position of indigenous groups who straddle international borders and therefore share cultural and historical backgrounds that transcend national identities. The Ojibwa, for example, are a transnational ethnic group with a presence in both the United States and Canada. Describing the Ojibwa as primarily a Canadian First Nation or an American Indian tribe bars our view of the Ojibwa as a distinct ethnic group with a foot on both sides of the Sault Sainte Marie River, effectively adding a national-political barrier on top of a geographical barrier to Pan-Ojibwa identity. While the Ojibwa in Canada and the United States possess distinct national identities, both groups share a similarly themed history regarding colonizing entities and an ethnic history and worldview that in many central ways transcend national identities, spaces, and histories.

Despite efforts to reduce or avoid generalizations, however, we cannot deny the common features of history amongst indigenous groups as a whole—warfare, colonialism, racism, abject poverty, preventable diseases of the mind and body, political marginalization, disruptions to social structure, loss of language, forced assimilation, and a dogged pursuit of political self-determination and cultural revitalization. Indigenous or non-Western peoples also share a cosmology or worldview characterized by a spiritual, holistic outlook on nature, self, community, social structure, life, death, sickness, health, and other major components of the human experience. More general descriptions of youth suicide in indigenous communities, then, are at times justified when conclusions or evidence concerning youth suicide touches on basic historical and cultural similarities. The boarding school era, for instance, is an extremely significant historical event for indigenous communities across the United States and Canada that greatly disrupted indigenous ways of life by attempting to replace indigenous identity and social structure with White Euro-American identity. The impact of boarding schools on an indigenous person's sense of identity and social cohesion, and the psychological effect of traumatic experiences associated with boarding schools, may become a potential risk factor for suicidal ideation amongst indigenous peoples as a whole.

In order to avoid generalization and to acknowledge the cultural, political, and historical meanings of the title(s) of the community at the center of this work, I identify the community via several titles—Anishnaabek, Ojibwa, Bowheting Ojibwa or Anishnaabek, and Sault Tribe. Each title corresponds with a revolving door of social, historical, ethnic, and political contexts experienced by community members. When differentiating between indigenous individuals and non-indigenous people living in or around the Sault Tribe community, I will use the term "Tribal" and "non-Tribal." The term "indigenous" references sources on indigenous peoples or Native Americans generally or when discussing a feature of youth suicide or behavioral health specific to the Sault Tribe that can reasonably be associated with indigenous history as a whole.

Audience

In a similar spirit of the work of Great Lakes Native American historian Charles Cleland, this book is written for the "interested lay reader" (Cleland, 2000) as well as social scientists, public health workers, and those in a position to implement suicide prevention and intervention policies and approaches in indigenous communities. Social scientists usually report findings to purely academic audiences according to scholarly format, which is understandable given that scholarly debate is essential to development of research on health disparities. We must not forget, however, to treat communities affected mentally and physically by harmful social issues as partners with an equal, if not more than equal, stake in receiving actionable information to more effectively combat health disparities.

Keeping both the lay and specialist audiences in mind, this book is an attempt at speaking with and for community members in the hopes that individuals, families, and leaders can add this work to their own views and observations on indigenous youth suicide. Throughout this work, I elaborate on specific terminology and aspects of the research process, providing definitions (mostly provided in my own words) and drawing analogies not usually included in scholarly works. Creative ethnographic writing further serves to connect research results to everyday situations and stimulate an empathetic response amongst both scholars and lay people.

That being said, it may be suitable to briefly describe what cultural anthropology is, in my own words, and what a cultural anthropologist tries to accomplish for those not familiar with the methods and purposes of the discipline of cultural anthropology. Cultural anthropologists try to gain a deep knowledge and appreciation for the values, attitudes, beliefs, language, history, and traditions of specific social or ethnic groups by observing everyday interactions between people and their environments—the specific culture of that group. Cultural anthropologists also try to compare and contrast the cultures of multiple groups, including past civilizations (through material evidence and written histories), to understand human culture as a whole. In order to more easily tell the difference between individual cultures and human culture as a whole (in my humble opinion), you could refer to individual cultures as little 'c' and human culture as the big 'C,' 'c/C' standing for 'culture.'

We become members of a distinct cultural group (little 'c') by learning behaviors and inheriting values from family, friends, and community—a process called enculturation. In this way, we inherit a cultural identity, or a sense of self and community values that we build upon and eventually pass on to future generations. The ways that one can observe and understand culture are countless. The interactions that take place between individuals, groups, people, the objects we use every day, and humans' manipulation of the environment all tell us something about our learned and shared values.

Anthropologists specialize in understanding how people express their ethnic identity and values, the development of culture, by immersing themselves within specific ethnic groups. The term for this process of immersion in the daily life of an ethnic group is 'participant observation.' During participant observation, anthropologists pay attention to everyday interactions and listen attentively to individuals during conversations and interviews. In essence, cultural anthropologists re-learn, as best they can, a language, social systems, a worldview, and set of values. When anthropologists review the information they gathered, they can focus on general and specific topics, themes, and patterns expressed by the behaviors and experiences they observed in the community, and in some ways, within themselves.

Pursuing an understanding of living cultures is usually the domain of cultural anthropologists; also called 'ethnographers'—'ethno' meaning 'culture,' and 'graph' meaning 'a measurement of.' In reality, ethnography or cultural anthropology is something that anyone can accomplish because humans naturally, and necessarily, observe each other on a constant basis in order to be more aware of their environment and to make choices that are more effective. Topics of ethnographic study are limitless, ranging from gender, sexuality, government, conflict, language, food and diet to health, music, age, economy, trade, and spirituality. The topic of this short ethnographic work is youth suicide in an Ojibwa community.

Government, Demographics, and Economy; Maps, Local and Regional

In 1979, after years of lobbying, the United States federal government recognized the Ojibwa residents of Sugar Island and the American side of the Sault Sainte Marie River as the Sault Sainte Marie Tribe of Chippewa Indians. The Sault Tribe reservation (proper) occupies the eastern side of Sault Sainte Marie, Michigan, which is one of two population centers that could qualify as "urban" in Michigan's Upper Peninsula (the other being Marquette towards the western side of the Upper Peninsula). The Sault Tribe considers the eastern half of the Upper Peninsula original lands or areas historically populated by the Sault Tribe ancestors, including Marquette, Delta, Alger, Schoolcraft, Luce, Chippewa, and Mackinac counties. These counties are referred to as the "Seven County Service Area," where the Sault Tribe has established trust lands, housing areas, service centers, health clinics, and business enterprises, embedded in public schools to provide extra services for Tribal students and other administrative offices.

The Seven County Service Area is divided into five "units," each electing representatives proportionate to the unit population (one to four representatives, respectively). Representatives sit on a Tribal Board of Directors headed by an elected Tribal Chairperson. Governmental and economic subjects, such as the Tribal constitution, government structure-restructuring and Tribal management of enterprises, contracts with private and non-Tribal government entities, and utilization of treaty rights and federal resources are sources of recent and ongoing debate amongst Sault Tribe members. While Sault Tribe members live throughout the state of Michigan and the Great Lakes region, the Seven County Service Area holds roughly 30 percent of the Sault Tribe's over 40,000 members (Sault Tribe Office of Planning and Development, email communication, 2017). The Sault Tribe is a member of the Inter-Tribal Council of Michigan, a non-profit, non-governmental advocacy and resource agency that represents and serves eleven of twelve federally recognized tribes residing in Michigan's Upper and Lower Peninsula.

Map of Michigan with major population centers and Great Lakes international waterway border

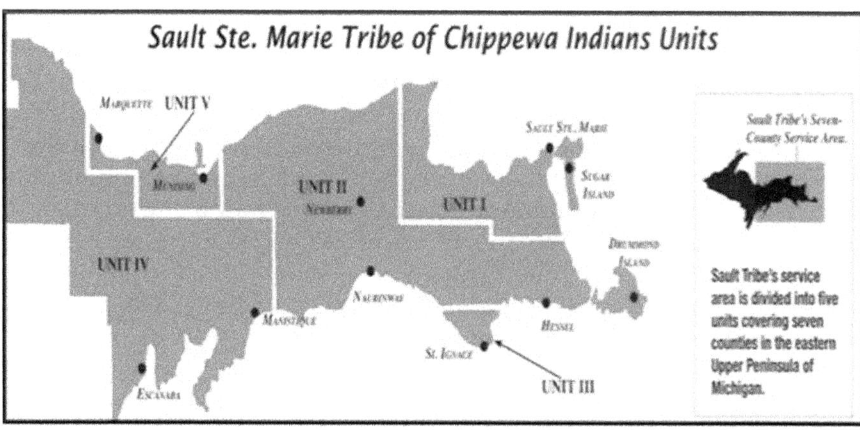

Seven County Service Area map, Sault Sainte Marie Tribe of Chippewa Indians (saulttribe.com)

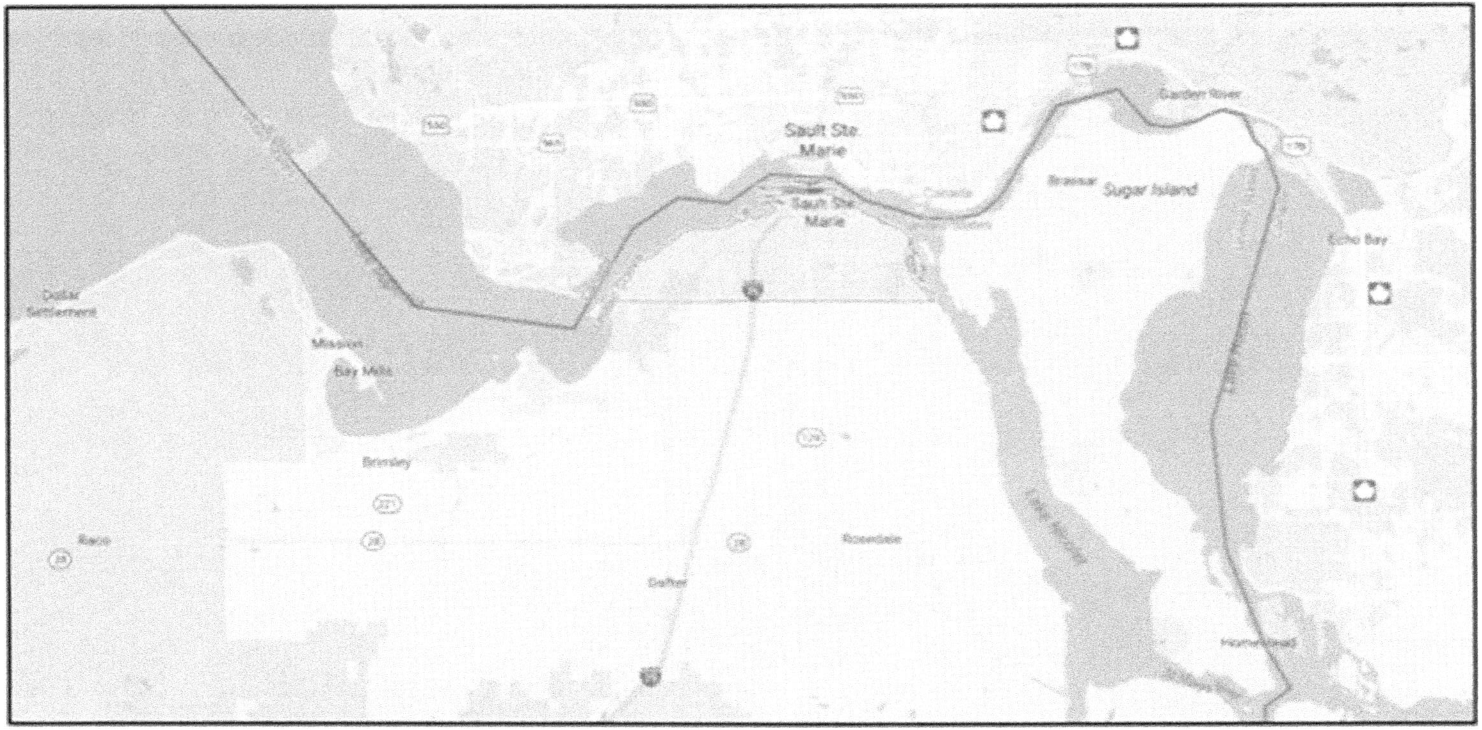

Sault Sainte Marie, Michigan (highlighted) and surrounding area (Google Maps)

Sault Sainte Marie, Michigan and surrounding area, satellite image (Google Maps)

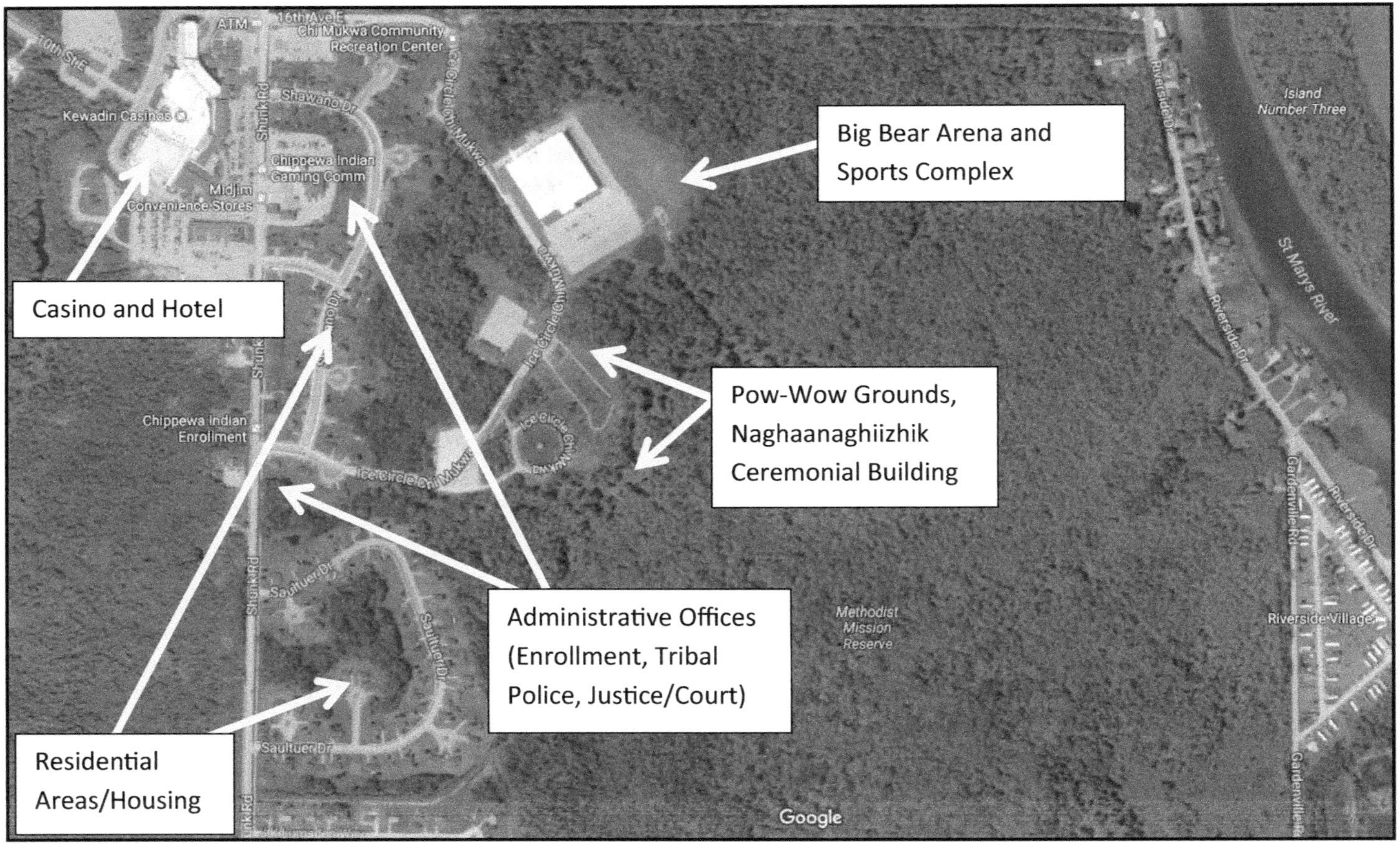

Sault Tribe reservation proper, key areas (Google Maps)

The sky is gray. I cannot feel the temperature, but I sense that it is cold. The earth is covered in dying weeds and brush, and interspersed with sickly trees. I notice a machine within arm's reach. At that moment, a voice speaks to me—"that one is the fastest."

Glancing up from the machine, I see a man in dark clothing with no face.

"That one is the fastest. It's faster than all the others."

Climbing on the machine, I waste no time in opening the throttle and speeding down the dirt track.

Faster, faster, faster. . . . Speeding past torn up fields of the same sickly brown hue. I lose control of the machine. Or to be more accurate, it takes control. It follows a path cut through the forest as if by a razor's edge. I clutch the handles, trying to wrest control from the machine. Control over this Thing is impossible, and as I give up I see other people riding machines with abandon over the torn up Earth, through fields where crops might have grown once. When will this be over?

Suddenly, I am flying forward above the ground. The Machine, the torn up fields with their dead trees and sickly vegetation, the people who think they are controlling the Machines that are controlling them . . . and the cold. The world transitions into warmth. My feet land lightly on a path of soft, dark, rich Earth. As I begin to walk forward in this new space, a sweet wind hits my face. The same wind combs through the lush green grasses growing tall on both sides of the path, and the grass dances in return. Beautiful, ancient trees at a distance hem in the rolling fields that stretch out around me. A long, stone house appears on the left. Two stories tall, the stone house displays many windows for its many rooms.

Traveling to the back of the house, I am surprised to see my grandmother standing by a set of wooden chairs and a table. She wears a simple blue dress. Is this her house?

From our vantage point, great fields of lush grass radiate out to the tree line. The color of the sky is blue bird egg.

"What a great house you have grandma" I say.

I hear no response. I turn my head and see that she is no longer standing by the chairs. Casting my eyes about, I spot her at the rear wall of the stone house. Why is she picking at the walls?

I wonder if there is something wrong with the house. I see pieces of stone and mortar crumble in her hands.

'Yes'—she thinks back to me.

Before I can ask what is wrong with her home, I hear her say in my mind—'Remember the Indian Room.'

Without thinking, I look up to a room in the second story of the house. Through the window, a light is glowing softly, faintly from within. Before I can investigate the source of light and the room that harbors it, I wake.

Stories

Stories Kill,
Stories Create,
Stories Imprison
And Liberate

Stories can strike,
Stories can fall,
Stories are wielded
By us all

What can we do
With the stories we tell?
But see one of heaven
Or live one of hell?

1 Introduction

Author's Approach

Rates, methods of suicide (e.g., firearm, overdose, strangulation), gender disparities (male-female ratio of completions/attempts), and other patterns of suicide amongst indigenous people of the United States and Canada vary widely according to region and ethnic group (MacNeil, 2008; Strickland, 1996). Generally speaking, however, indigenous peoples residing in both countries display suicide rates significantly higher than the national average—1.5 times higher than the national average in the United States (CDC, 2013), 5 to 7 times the national average in Canada (Health Canada, 2013), and in the case of the Inuit of Canada, 11 times the national average (Health Canada, 2013). As alarming as these statistics are, accurate data on indigenous youth suicide remains clouded by ineffective reporting procedures. While numerous factors, "socioeconomic characteristics, substance abuse, barriers to mental health services and acculturation play a role in the occurrence of" indigenous youth suicide, more effective measurement and reporting procedures are required to accurately gauge indigenous youth suicide at local, regional, and national levels (Olson and Wahab, 2006).

Indigenous youth suicide has been the focus of media attention, public outcry, multidisciplinary research, and to an extent, government attention for nearly half a century—arguably making indigenous youth suicide one of the longest lasting public health issues in the United States and Canada. The immediate reaction to youth suicide, in public and academic circles, often stems from two basic questions: Why did they do it? What could we have done to prevent it? The purpose of answering these questions is to prevent future suicides from taking place. The only component of the story that seems to be missing, then, would be the answer as to why youth suicide occurs in such high numbers within indigenous communities.

I started on my own path toward exploring such questions nearly ten years ago, while visiting friends and family in Sault Sainte Marie, Michigan. Community members voiced great concern over youth suicide and the behavioral and spiritual health of youth. Each discussion exposed the heartbreaking and complex nature of youth suicide, which frustrates the search for answers. Years later, as a graduate student of anthropology at Western Michigan University, I chose to tackle the issue of youth suicide in the Sault Tribe by conducting a case study, with the goal of exploring the history, impact, and cultural complexities surrounding youth suicide in the Sault Tribe, while outlining potential remedies for this destructive issue.

In order to grasp the community's views on and experiences with suicide and related health topics, I lived in the Sault Sainte Marie area and took part in everyday activities and community events. Research also relied on structured interviews with professionals serving in the areas of education and youth development, medicine, mental health, social work, traditional medicine, government-tribal political policy related to tribal youth, non-tribal youth, and families. This work refers to interviewees as "administrators"—"educational administrators," "Sault Area Schools administrators," "mental health administrators," and similar general titles that help ensure the confidentiality of participants' involvement. Confidentiality is a key component of ethnographic research, as it allows participants the freedom to discuss views and information that may be sensitive without fear of backlash from the community. Youth under the age of 18 were not included in interviews. However, informal discussions with individuals and groups of Ojibwa youth took place on several occasions, while interactions between youth and community were observed and noted, adding necessary context to this study.

While the inclusion of interview participants was solely based on status as "administrators," many interviewees are themselves Tribal members, parents of Tribal youth, otherwise related to Tribal members (spouse, in-law), long-term residents of the Eastern Upper Peninsula area, or possess a combination of such backgrounds. As a result, the familial links, local knowledge, and personal-emotional investment in the future of Tribal youth allowed interviewees to speak passionately, and at times emotionally, of their views, observations, and firsthand experiences with Tribal youth and families. The consistency of Tribal backgrounds and Tribally centered backgrounds amongst participants ensured that the views, beliefs, and experiences of the Tribal community, as well as views of the Tribal community, remained central in this work.

Interview participants shared documents and reports (e.g., student surveys, government reports and articles, grant application information), while pointing out various resources that further guided this study. The shared documents and information added to collected government documents, gray literature (e.g., organizational language found on websites or in regulatory guidelines), visual representation of culture, recorded in still photos, video, and field notes describing visual representations of culture and other primary sources that provide a firsthand account of attitudes and contexts surrounding suicide. Throughout my time in 'the Soo,' I spoke informally with Tribal and non-Tribal members of various ages and backgrounds about the issue of youth suicide and related topics. The resulting informal conversations and encounters with elders, teenagers, and visitors from outside the community (unstructured interviews) heavily inform this work.

While the larger case study framework relied on interviews, participant observation, and collection and analysis of documents, this study relied greatly on historical and anthropological literature on the Ojibwa and the Anishnaabek (e.g., Cleland, 2001, 1992; Jackson, 2002). The type and combination of methods used in this case study are designed to create the opportunity for information and views, previously unexpressed, to surface in the academic and public arena. In the sense that this work offers previously unexpressed views, information, and forms of evidence; challenges the current views on youth suicide and the cultural and historical realities of mental health in indigenous communities; and combines historical and anthropological methods in order to understand historical developments and cultural interaction (Barber and Berdan, 1998), the work is most accurately presented as an ethnohistorical case study.

Critique of Anthropology

Despite significant participation and community interest in this research, I was ever conscious of the conflicted relationship between anthropology (and the social sciences in general) and indigenous peoples. From the late 1900s to the mid-1900s, early American anthropologists spent a majority of their professional experience in indigenous communities, where they collected artifacts and recorded oral histories, traditions, music, language, and, using video and still photography, the dances of Tribal peoples. Anthropologists hurriedly recorded and collected such aspects of indigenous culture in an effort to preserve the history and memory of what they saw as the 'dying Indian.' Speaking on the conflicted relationship between Native America and anthropology, Orin Starn (2011) describes this early period of anthropology:

> It can be easy to forget just how central Native Americans once were to U.S. anthropology; Papa Franz [a central figure of early American anthropology] and virtually all his students fanned out into Indian country like a second invading army, this time armed with notebooks and seizing not territory but instead information about myths, rituals, and kinship systems. Even those better known for work in other places like Margaret Mead in Samoa, also did research and published about Native Americans, the Omaha in Mead's case. . . .

> When I worked on the Navajo reservation back in the late 1970s, you still heard a bad joke that indexed the reservation ubiquity of anthropologists; "How many people are there in a Navajo family?" "Five—mother, father, two children . . . and an anthropologist."
>
> (180)

The early- to mid-twentieth-century rush to study and preserve tribal ways of life became known as 'salvage ethnography.' Written observations, measurements, audio and video recordings, artwork and artifacts were represented in scientific journals and museum exhibits that perpetuated the Western view of Tribal peoples as primitive groups—as lower, less developed forms of human society compared with white, Euro-American society (e.g., Morgan's Theories on Social Evolution). The status of primitive races as dying and in need of caretaking justified the paternal relationship that Western government and society forced upon indigenous peoples. Anthropologists extremely critical of their own discipline's complicity in the treatment of indigenous peoples often refer to anthropology at this time as a 'handmaiden of colonialism' or a "child of Western imperialism" (Gough, 1968: 12). Responding to such charges and reflecting on the lessons of history, anthropologists hold participant rights and the potential dangers of ethnographic study as an essential component of training, education, and research considerations. Despite the many advances that Tribal communities have made toward self-determination, Tribal communities continue the struggle to achieve an equal role in the writing of ethnic and national histories and regain control and protections of artifacts and historically significant places. To this day, disturbing images of anthropologists digging (sometimes literally, in the case of archaeologists) into the historical, traditional, and physical identity of indigenous peoples obstruct the creation of trusting relationships between Tribal communities and social scientists.

Despite my status as a (budding) anthropologist and the use of Western research methods, nothing could replace the fact that I am a member of the very group experiencing the behavioral phenomena I am attempting to understand. Throughout the research process, I realized that my family shares a similar history with those who faced and continue to face the threat of youth suicide. When setting out to investigate youth suicide, it was with the hope that my connection to the people, places, memories, and history of the Sault Tribe would minimize any sense of distrust arising from my role as an anthropologist, while simultaneously fostering a mutual relationship based on shared connections and experiences. The unique ability of an indigenous anthropologist to gather and ingest information that may otherwise not be available or fully disclosed to an 'outsider' is powerfully described by Zora Neale Hurston in *Mules and Men* (1935), a study of African American folklore in her hometown of

Eatonville, Florida. Her experiences collecting stories and folklore shed light on the unique impact that being a daughter of Eatonville had on her assignment and interactions with community members—a situation that Hurston ruminates on throughout her work:

> Folklore is not as easy to collect as it sounds. The best source is where there are the least outside influences and these people, being usually underprivileged, are the shyest. They are most reluctant at times to reveal that which the soul lives by. And the Negro, in spite of his open-faced laughter, his seeming acquiescence, is particularly evasive. You see we are a polite people and we do not say to our questioner, "Get out of here!" We smile and tell him or her something that satisfies the white person because, knowing so little about us, he doesn't know what he is missing. The Indian resists curiosity by a stony silence. The Negro offers a feather-bed resistance. That is, we let the probe enter, but it never comes out. It gets smothered under a lot of laughter and pleasantries.
>
> The theory behind our tactics: "The white man is always trying to know into somebody else's business. All right, I'll set something outside the door of my mind for him to play with and handle. He can read my writing but he sho' can't read my mind. I'll put this play toy in his hand, and he will seize it and go away. Then I'll say my say and sing my song."
>
> (2, 3)

In much the same vein that the curious "white man who is always trying to know into somebody else's business" is rebuffed with "stony silence" or a "feather-bed resistance" built around polite half-truths and jest, the non-indigenous anthropologists may find certain thoughts, beliefs, and attitudes of indigenous peoples inaccessible. Participants and community members aware of the study displayed openness through sharing of intimate experiences, personal views, and even unpopular opinions; an openness further underscored by the sensitive nature of the topic of research. Perhaps for the same reason that Zora received such blunt and revealing information in her quest for understanding, my status as an Ojibwa man opened the door to a more nuanced understanding of youth suicide in the Sault Tribe.

Adversely, my identity as an indigenous person may cause Western social scientists to question, openly or introspectively, the accuracy of my representation of research results and the value of this work. A goal of social science—a goal of science in general—is to collect evidence and present interpretations and conclusions based on an analysis of the evidence. The validity and usefulness of conclusions rely on the investigator's ability to practice objectivity or maintain a sense of detachment from the subject of study. Personal, political, or emotional forms of attachment to the object of study could compromise the collection of information (i.e., frame questions to lead to a presumed conclusion) or influence a biased presentation of research results (favoring specific aspects of the research while sidelining other data).

Regardless of the absence or presence of prevailing bias as a result of my personal attachment to the community, the extended claim that my added status as community member provides further value to the study may be questioned. In essence, if I am using 'traditional' social science methods (participant observation, interviews, document analysis), what extra value could be added by me being an indigenous person? However, the place I occupy as a community member and anthropologist favors a vantage point far too absent from research—that of the indigenous person—a sentiment shared by the community. While preparing fish for the feast at the Sugar Island Pow-Wow, I asked Cecil Pavlat, a retired Sault Tribe NAGPRA (Native American Graves Repatriation Act) representative and respected community member, his views on anthropologists, historians, and social scientists. He paused in thought, holding a freshly floured filet of whitefish above the hot oil, and said, "Anthropologists think that they can tell our story, but they can't. I think it's about time we had our own anthropologists." With such words in mind, I join a growing number of indigenous anthropologists like Minnesota Ojibwa Sonya Atalay, who conducts cultural research "for, with and by" the community' (Atalay, 2012: Preface).

My connection to the Sault Tribe also provides one of the three key components to a story—purpose. The purpose or goal of this work is to enhance the health, happiness, and future of not only the community, but of my own family. I have found, when returning to the question of whether or not I can remain objective in the context of research that includes my community and, in many ways, my family history, that the purpose of this work reinforces urgency for objectivity rather than eroding it. Use of analogy can help explain and elaborate on this point.

A medical doctor, essentially a scientist of the human body, must view the patient objectively in order to interpret symptoms and understand an ailment and its causes. Once the ailment and the causes are recognized, the doctor attempts to heal or 'fix' the patient. The doctor's extensive education in human biology and basic use of the scientific method makes the process of examination and treatment easier. The social relationship that exists between the doctor (scientist, authority figure) and patient (object, subordinate) may help the doctor approach the patient without emotion or distraction. However, what happens when the doctor approaches the operating table, only to find his or her own child?

Initially, the doctor may be overcome with grief and anxiety caused by emotional connection to the person lying before him or her. The doctor is no longer a scientist of the human body, and the patient no longer an object of medical study and treatment—the relationship is now subjective. Can a subjective relationship, in this scenario, help the doctor to focus and increase the likelihood that the child will live? Would a parent, with the ability, knowledge, and opportunity to save the life of a child, operate with as much or more care, concentration, skill, and devotion than a physician not so invested? Add to the investment intimate knowledge of the history of the patient and potential complications—allergies, previous injuries, strengths and weaknesses. The emotional investment of the parent-doctor/child-patient relationship may motivate the most direct, effective treatment, even if painful, to support the life of the patient.

Much like the parent-doctor looking down on the operating table, as a social scientist I look down at reports, rates, tables, field notes, interview transcripts and see the immediate and long-term future of those I love—my son, nephews, nieces, and the future generations of my family and people. Instead of creating a biased approach or an overly subjective connection to the research, I find myself motivated to seek answers to the issues revolving around youth suicide more directly and effectively. I see my identity as an Ojibwa man and my intimate knowledge of the places, practices, and history of Bowheting not as an obstacle, but as source of great insight when attempting to understand the history, meanings, and effects of youth suicide in the Sault Tribe.

Beyond the powerful nuance of the researcher being a member of the community, a balancing act of sorts exists in this work, in that two aims of this book are to (1) report the results of research and (2) examine how to conduct culturally appropriate research, largely from the perspective of an indigenous scholar. These two goals, however, need not be competing in that the former must overshadow the latter or vice versa, in order to make a clear and purposeful contribution to current research and clinical approaches in the field of mental health in indigenous communities. Treating and conducting research on health disparities in indigenous populations requires culturally appropriate methods and mentalities on behalf of the research and health care communities (Goodkind et al., 2015). In this case, the examination of research methods and process, as well as reporting of results, are considered mutual goals that can lead to culturally appropriate research, while providing a platform for debate and critical discussion from the classroom to the research community and the public policy sphere. This mission is a central goal of this work. In any case, the balance between an examination of current methods with the intention of creating culturally informed health care approaches, and the generation of purely descriptive research results, is precarious—and one cannot and need not be separated from the other.

Theoretical Overview of Indigenous Youth Suicide

Most studies of indigenous youth suicide, until recently, have been quantitative (Kral, 2012). Quantitative research includes collecting statistical data on behaviors within human populations and running the collected information through mathematical formulas in order to uncover patterns of behavior. Afterward, quantitative researchers create charts, graphs, tables, and other statistical models that visually display specific themes and patterns of human behavior (e.g., pie charts, bar graphs). Perhaps the most common area of data collection in indigenous youth suicide research regards type and number of 'risk factors' that a Tribal youth is exposed to or exhibits.

Risk factors are specific features of an individual's personal background that may affect suicidal thinking, and possible suicide attempt or completion. Examples of risk factors are personal, family, or psychological history (existing mental disorder, dysfunctional family settings), the surrounding environments (home life, poor neighborhood), or types of activities one engages in (substance abuse). While risk factors are specific to individual communities, certain risk factors are more common across indigenous communities, such as alcohol and substance abuse (e.g., Allen et al., 2014; Barlow et al., 2012) or a previous history of suicide attempts. According to a study of ninth- to twelfth-grade AI/AN students attending Bureau of Indian Affairs–funded schools who attempted suicide, Shaughnessy et al (2004) found that suicide attempts were associated with

> depression, substance use, availability of firearms, sexual activity, and a history of violence, both as victim and perpetrator. Among AI/AN youth specifically, suicide attempts also are associated with poor school performance, poor physical health status, families or friends with a history of suicide attempts and/or suicide completions, family disconnectedness, physical abuse, and sexual abuse.
>
> (177)

The rise of specific risk factors, however, may coincide with a state of depression, caused by an underlying sense of helplessness. Studying the relationship between alcohol use, excessive alcohol use (binge drinking), drinking to cope, hopelessness, and depressive symptoms in First Nations communities, Stewart (2011) found that "(a) hopelessness was directly linked to depressive symptoms, (b) depressive symptoms were directly linked to drinking to cope, and (c) drinking to cope was directly linked to excessive drinking" (5). The perpetuation of this destructive cycle is explained through the theory of self-medication, "which posits that depressed individuals drink to reduce negative emotions, and are thus at risk for heavier drinking and more alcohol-related problems as a consequence" (Ibid., 2).

The effect of hopelessness, or the sense of learned helplessness resulting from continued exposure to stress and anxiety without alleviation, escape, or perceived route of escape, is a salient issue in indigenous youth suicide studies. Research, (largely contributed to the work of Aaron Beck), indicates that hopelessness is an effective predictor of future suicide attempts (Kovacs, Beck and Weissman, 1975, Beck, Brown and Steer (1989). As Stewart explains:

> [D]iscrimination, disruptions to family connections, geographic dislocation, and abject poverty arising from colonial policies have resulted in social and economic circumstances which are often objectively bleak for Canadian Aboriginal people, setting the stage for the development of hopelessness.
>
> (6, 14)

In communities experiencing risk factors and underlying forces such as hopelessness, suicide does not fall evenly on the indigenous youth. Subsets of youth show higher prevalence of suicide ideation, attempts, or completions. Young males, for instance, complete suicide at higher rates than young females, while females attempt suicide at up to five times the rate of young males, and those in the sexual minority are more likely to attempt suicide than heterosexual youth (Mackin, 2012). Higher suicide completion rates for males is especially a historical reality, as displayed by earlier analyses of indigenous youth suicide (e.g., May and Dizmang, 1974; Shore, 1975).

While risk factors have been a dominant point of focus for suicide studies, two other factors—protective factors and resilience—are increasingly relevant to suicidology and suicide prevention studies. Protective factors and resilience are defined here as aspects of a youth's background and environment that may reduce the chances that a person will attempt suicide, and the ability to 'bounce back' from a potentially harmful or unhealthy event or situation, respectively. While understanding the risk factors for youth suicide is essential in creating effective prevention and intervention programs, stressing the negative aspects of an indigenous youth's life experiences may dismiss the protective, healthy areas of a young person's personal background, character, the healthful effects of activities that he or she engages in, to include the healing aspects of the indigenous culture. Whether introducing new sensory experiences (sitting on a balance ball in a classroom) to create a more enjoyable learning environment (Grewal and Porter, 2007) or recognizing the role of family connectedness and involvement in traditional activities (Tingey et al., 2014), exploring areas of young people's lives that can be or already are a source of protection or resilience-building can lead to effective suicide prevention and intervention.

Protective factors may also provide what Mackin, Perkins, and Furrer (2012) describe as a "buffering effect," which takes place when healthy features present in one's lifestyle counteract risk factors. Availability of extended family as a source of comfort, for example, may buffer against extreme poverty and sense of helplessness. Examining the combined impact of risk and protective factors can reveal a "risk threshold," or a critical balancing point where, depending on the number and type of risk and protective factors present, youth may sway between a sense of anxiety or suicidal thinking and active contemplation and eventual suicide attempt. Aware of the specific protective and risk factors influencing the risk threshold, indigenous communities with limited resources can more strategically augment intervention or prevention programs.

Pettingell et al (2008) similarly included a "resilience paradigm" that "identified the strongest risk and protective factors relative to a past suicide attempt among girls and boys." According to Pettingell et al,

> The resilience paradigm gives salience to critical aspects, called assets, strengths, or protective factors, within young people's lives that buffer against a wide array of risks, health-jeopardizing behaviors, or negative outcomes. Considered within an ecological framework, these risk and protective factors can have environmental (e.g., family functioning, peer norms, school climate), behavioral (e.g., competence, coping skills, behavioral repertoire), or personal (e.g., cognitions, self-beliefs, connectedness with others) origins. . . . Then, in this analysis, the statistically robust risk and protective factors were examined in combination to predict the likelihood of a history of a suicide attempt in this sample of urban American Indian youth. Our overarching hypothesis was that protective factors derived from the resiliency paradigm would substantially offset the risk factors associated with suicide attempts.
>
> (466)

What Pettingell et al and Mackin recognize through their respective studies is that focusing on risks to the individual or a 'problems' centered approach threatens to overshadow the positive features of indigenous lifestyle, or "assets" available to indigenous youth. Including wellness in the framework of youth suicide studies, or as a measurable trait, has the added benefit of resonating with indigenous views of health and treatment, while increasing the effectiveness of prevention-intervention (Ibid.; Mackin, Perkins, and Furrer, 2012; Sahota and Kastelic, 2014).

Indigenous youth suicide is rarely analyzed as a personal, historical, or cultural narrative, in the way that medical anthropologists write of social embodiments of disease (Sontag, reprint 1978), the illness-sickness roles that exist within "medical systems as cultural systems" (Kleinmen,

1978), organs, the human body, biological processes, and conceptualizations of death (Lock, 2002) or cultural conflicts that take place over ideas of health, medicine, and treatment (Fadiman, reprint 2012). Medical anthropologists investigating the formation and expansion of health disparities developed useful explanatory models outlining the impact of cultural change and maladaptation, social structure and social forces (stigma), and formation of oppressive ideology on development of health care systems and treatment (e.g., Howard and Millard, 1997). While youth suicide studies remain largely quantitative, medical anthropology, with its emphasis on the cultural or ideological views of health and treatment, bring a nuanced qualitative approach to bear on the topic of youth suicide.

Qualitative research may be difficult to define, as there are many approaches to defining qualitative research. Qualitative research studies the quality or unique characteristics of the object under study. (Quantitative research can mean the collection of statistics or the statistical evaluation of a set of data.) The difference in qualitative and quantitative approaches lies in the methods used to answer similar questions. A quantitative approach may ask how many youths complete suicide, the rate that youths are exposed to risk or protective factors, or how many indigenous youths feel suicidal when drinking alcohol or using substances. In a qualitative study (such as this), more descriptive questions are pursued. Why do youths attempt suicide? What is the relationship between suicide and substance abuse? What leads a youth toward attempting or completing, or being resilient to suicide? While this study emphasizes the meanings or the conditions surrounding youth suicide, both quantitative and qualitative studies attempt to uncover general and specific patterns of youth suicide while seeking out potential causes and remedies.

The overwhelming reliance on statistics or a numbers-driven description of youth suicide, however, produces a picture of indigenous youth and their communities devoid of the color of life experiences, feelings, and personal and community histories. In essence, indigenous voices count as statistical "data"—not represented directly in research texts as people speaking directly to underlying causes. Qualitative research, on the other hand, delves more intimately into the human condition by describing everyday lived experiences of individuals, communities, and cultures. In the case of indigenous youth suicide, qualitative research can help account for unique aspects of indigenous culture, lifestyle, and history that may influence youth suicide rates.

Thorough understanding of identity, a highly nuanced topic in indigenous cultural studies, for example, requires the use of qualitative methods. Indigenous people identify as "indigenous," "Tribal," "Indian," or as members of specific ethnic-Tribal groups in a number of ways—through genealogical ties to distant ancestors, via practice of manners, customs, language, and traditions, as a member of a political entity with a Tribal identification card providing evidence of membership, or a combination thereof. A statistical approach by itself, however, does not allow for an in-depth understanding of identity, or how indigenous people identify themselves as a member of a distinct ethnic group or member of 'Pan-Indian' culture, or the role of identity in indigenous youth suicide.

Edmonson's (2000) study of the relationship between suicide, hopelessness, self-efficacy, and powerlessness provides an example. Following a similar theme of quantitative studies of indigenous youth suicide, Edmonson recruited "American Indian" participants from Tribal clinics in urban and rural areas of Oklahoma, while spending no time exploring what "American Indian" culture is, how participants expressed their identity, or how "American Indian" identity may affect survey responses. Edmonson assures the reader that his use of the snowball method (a method which relies on creating contacts that then lead to other contacts that can be included in the study (hence, the "snowball effect") ensured that all participants were "authentic" American Indians. Regardless of the methods used to enlist participants, Edmonson spends no time explaining or defining authenticity or "authentic American Indian." Edmonson's approach is representative of an overriding theme of studies of indigenous health disparities, where "[c]ulture, instead of being a complex aspect [in suicide research] . . . becomes very often the answer to one (demographic) question" (Colucci and Martin, 2007a: 198; cited in Kral (2012).

Not taking ethnic identity, or personal, sexual, gendered, geographical, generational, national, or a myriad of other qualitative traits into consideration adds to the overgeneralization of indigenous youth suicide and potential risk and protective factors. As a result, differences in suicide rates can be "muted when aggregated across regions" (Herne Bartholomew and Weahkee (2014).

Leaving ethnic identities and histories out of youth suicide studies abuses research to the fact that "American Indians" or "First Nations" comprise hundreds of diverse ethnic groups hailing from varying geographical areas, climates, ecosystems, and landscapes (urban, rural), operate in differing economic systems, possess distinct languages, dialects, manners, customs, histories, and retain separate views on life, death, suicide, and health. In a literature review, Goodkind et al. (2010) state policy recommendations for improving behavioral health amongst American Indians:

> When we address this sensitive issue, we cannot assume that all people share the same perspective. A very wide spectrum of beliefs among Native people, ranging from people who speak their Native language and follow traditional spiritual practices and values, to others who

> have a Native cultural identity but are Christian, to those who are fully immersed in the dominant culture and do not speak their native language or practice traditional religion exists. It is important for providers and systems to be aware of this diversity of beliefs and practices and to avoid assumptions.
>
> (6)

Aware of the dangers of ignoring inter-tribal differences and presenting indigenous peoples as a general racial-ethnic category suffering from mental health issues, early researchers warned of the potential stereotyping of what was called the "suicidal Indian" (Shore, 1975; McIntosh and Santos, 1980). Unfortunately, such warnings have largely gone unheeded and the overgeneralization of tribal health data and theoretical models on indigenous health restrict researchers from uncovering potential root causes for youth suicide. Overgeneralization of indigenous health issues, however, is not limited to research results.

Tribal mental health initiatives and suicide prevention programs are largely evidence-based treatment, as are national statistics, government research, and academic behavioral science research. Without understanding the context of studies cited in behavioral health programs, or a critical study of suicide in the individual community, however, treatments respond to nationally aggregated data and cultural contexts of distance communities, while ignoring the realities of a specific community. The pursuit of evidence-based treatment, in particular, leads mental health programs, schools, and communities to transplant treatment programs from community to community, despite geographical, cultural, and economic differences. For example, the Ojibwa of the Upper Midwest (characterized as both an urban and rural, reservation and off-reservation based, largely Christian population with a minority practicing indigenous religion) may implement prevention programming from the Apache of the Southwest US (rural, reservation based, mixed Christian and indigenous religion) without taking into consideration inter-tribal differences.

Social scientists and preventative care workers are realizing that youth suicide research and prevention require more qualitative approaches that take ethnic and community developments into consideration. MacNeil (2008) states:

> The literature suggests that only by considering the specific needs of the culture, community, and environment can intervention and prevention meet with success. . . . Limited data exist regarding the various contexts and life experience of Aboriginal youth thought to place them at risk for attempted or completed suicide.
>
> (1)

MacNeil's point that future research must address "the specific needs of the culture" and the "various contexts and life experience of Aboriginal youth" may be a response to the limitations of the WHO definition (used in her review as a standard) and her exposure to literature that lacks thorough understanding of the relative meanings of suicide for aboriginal communities. Similarly, Heme et al. (2014) reviewed data on AI/AN youth suicide between 1999 and 2009 using the World Health Organization definition of risk factors, as opposed to localized concepts of risk for suicide or health disparities in general. Works criticizing the implicit exclusion of indigenous cultural views, or indigenous theories regarding suicide, continue to abandon ethnographic information, or fail to include and operationalize ethnographic information, which is the most essential component of any study attempting to formulate a relativistic worldview on suicide, risk factors, protective factors, and prevention.

In a case study of suicide in three pastoralist East African societies, Straight et al. (2015) combine an impressive store of ethnographic field experience with mixed methods research to illustrate that "cultural values—examined through ethnographic methods—are crucial not just for the sake of theory but also for pragmatic solutions to public health dilemmas" (574). The treatment of suicide as an anthropological object and use of ethnographic detail allowed the researchers to contextualize suicide and psychosocial health more broadly, within contemporary inter-ethnic violence, political conflict, and cultural constraints on suicide (i.e., taboos). A valuable point of this study, however, lies with a call for anthropologists to recognize their role as the "outsider," and the resulting necessity for "deep engagement" with communities in order to contextualize quantitative data on suicide.

In one of the first qualitative studies of a designated population of AI/AN youth (as part of an established community participant based research [CPBR] project with the White Mountain Apache), Tingey et al. (2014) assert:

> Intervention with those at highest risk for suicide requires refining and organizing risk factors into coherent conceptual models that address common risk factors for suicide, *as well as those that might be specific to Native teens and their communities*. A variety of conceptual models of suicide have been developed with implications for suicide prevention, such as those that focus on psychopathology (Shaffer et al., 1996), sociology (Durkheim, 1897), cognition (Beck et al., 1985), and behavior (Linehan, 1993). However, none of these models have taken an ecological approach to understanding suicide, nor were they developed specifically by and for suicidal behavior as it is experienced in Native communities.

> Qualitative studies of youths who have attempted suicide could be useful in understanding relationships between variables identified by quantitative approaches and to hone an ecologically based, Native-specific suicide risk model. Applying such a model to understanding risk pathways to suicidal behavior among Native youths can enlighten culturally anchored prevention approaches that might be relevant to other Native communities with high suicide rates.
>
> Qualitative approaches are essential to deepening how we understand suicide risk unique to a community and for moving the suicide prevention field forward (Hjelmeland and Knizek, 2010; Leenaars, 2002).
>
> (1518–1519; italics added)

Rather than fall into a quantitative versus qualitative debate, however, we can pursue more effective research models by creating avenues for multiple, complementary approaches to youth suicide. In a call for mixed methods research, Kral, Links, and Bergmans (2012) remind us of the fact that "suicide remains without an adequate or accepted general theory that incorporates multiple disciplines and perspectives," while promoting the benefits of augmenting quantitative research with qualitative research (and vice versa). Mixed methods research relies on the integration of multiple methodologies and disciplinary backgrounds to further our understanding of the overlap between culture and suicide while testing the efficacy of prevention programs.

Traditionally, Western academics and mental health care providers have dominated research design, goals, and leadership roles in indigenous youth suicide studies and prevention, leading to the marginalization of indigenous ways of knowing, methods of studying human behavior, and views on health and wellness. In response to this power dynamic, CPBR attempts to reverse the exclusion of indigenous voices from the research process by including Tribal members (youth, elders, traditional healers, leaders) in the research and prevention process as co-creators and leaders of the research design and prevention-intervention process. CPBR often begins when indigenous communities initiate contact with researchers (through university or public health organizations) and request assistance and resources. The CPBR process emphasizes active information sharing between researcher and community. As a result, the researcher becomes aware of specific cultural considerations and community priorities, the value of data increases, and potential prevention-intervention programs may have greater impact.

Describing the effectiveness of the CPBR method in their study of the effects of sensory experiences on mood enhancement amongst reservation based AI/AN youth, Doll and Brady explain:

> Through the use of a CPBR approach, the community determined the research question, the approach, how the intervention was implemented, and the outcome measure. Implementing programming and research in Native American communities by an outsider comes with inherent creative and ethical challenges (Minkler, 2004). Project HOPE is an example of a successful, culturally appropriate program. Typically, collecting data in Native American communities is a challenge. The amount of data collected from this program is a testament to the benefits of CPBR approaches that follow a community-driven research agenda.
>
> (2013: 156)

Through qualitative, collaborative research, Walls, Hautala, and Hurley (2014) bring to bear the "silenced voices" of Tribal community leaders, mental health administrators, and elders, placing the experiences and views of indigenous peoples at the fore. Using an ecological approach and stress exposure framework, Walls, Hautala, and Hurley explore the impact of historical trauma on individual, family, and community stress levels, presenting historical trauma as "the persistent, intergenerational exposure and response to multiple traumatic events within communities (Brave Heart, 1999; Brave Heart and DeBruyn, 1998)" (Ibid. 49). Historical trauma may be "considered historical in that" traumatic events, memories, social pressures, and colonial practices of the past may cause emotional anxiety and perpetuate harmful social environments across generations (Ibid. 50). Participants in Walls, Hautala, and Hurley's study identified interpersonal, community-level, and meso-level factors contributing to youth suicide, supporting the conclusion that "the broad array of contemporary outcomes of historical trauma as multilevel in nature, affecting individuals, families, and communities" (Ibid. 50). The definitions and usage of historical trauma, however, are not without nuance or conflict. Neizen (2015), discussing Kirmayer, Gone, and Moses (2014) states:

> The "historical" origins of trauma are called into question by Kirmayer, Gone and Moses (2014), who find that ongoing structural violence more clearly illuminates the persistent suffering of indigenous peoples in the Americas. Applying the term "postcolonial" to the historical background of suicide is similar to use of the concept of historical trauma, though with a closer temporal focus.
>
> (107)

Focusing on historical trauma in general terms may prevent researchers and communities from shifting attention toward "the social dislocation brought about by colonial settlement" (Kral, 2012) and ongoing structural violence. Structural violence as understood and operationalized by Kral, and pursued in the body of this work, shares similarities with the approach of Farmer et al. (2006):

> The term "structural violence" is one way of describing social arrangements that put individuals and populations in harm's way. The arrangements are structural because they are embedded in the political and economic organization of our social world; they are violent because they cause injury to people (typically, not those responsible for perpetuating such inequalities). With few exceptions, clinicians are not trained to understand such social forces, nor are we trained to alter them. Yet it has long been clear that many medical and public health interventions will fail if we are unable to understand the social determinants of disease.
>
> (1)

Structural violence, symbolic violence, and continued colonial (post-colonial implies that colonial relationships are in the past) are increasingly recognized as principal conditions for health disparities in indigenous communities (Mcgregor et al., 2011).

Current trends in suicidology include development of theoretical approaches beyond those introduced by Emile Durkheim. As historically indebted as suicidology is to Emile Durkheim, the French sociologist credited with the first comprehensive study on the topic of suicide, methodology and current theoretical approaches to indigenous youth suicide research are unduly limited by his work and early theories regarding suicidal behavior and suicide ideation. Durkheim (1951) painted a picture of suicide as an event dependent on the ebb and flow of social cohesion and sense of social solidarity in one's life (very simply put). According to Neizen's (2015) review of the work of French contemporary Gabrielle Tarde, Durkheim overemphasized the obvious forms of social cohesion (e.g., membership in a group or institution, exclusion from groups, strong or weak family bonds, religion) to the detriment of understanding other forces effecting suicidal ideation.

Tarde insisted that we must know how society coheres, rather than simply note the existence and effects of social cohesion on an individual's mental state. Tarde critiqued Durkheim for espousing a sociology of mythical or fictitious concepts, in that the social institutions Durkheim relied upon for measurements of social solidarity are invented by societies, and vary from culture to culture (Ibid. 105). Tarde, on the other hand, believed that suicide is largely affected by the forces of imitation and communication of ideas, imagery, and identity; forces which are more universally applicable to cultures than specific types of social institutions (developed along a Euro-American framework). Such emphasis on identity, symbols, and the construction and transmission of self and group image-identity and control over one's future is especially useful when attempting to understand behaviors in indigenous communities. The complex and often-confusing state of ethnic identity, beset by historical trauma, structural violence, symbolic violence, and struggles for self-determination and cultural continuity, and played out via symbols *and* demonstrations of social cohesion, continue to play a major role in the state of mental health and illness in indigenous communities (e.g., Kraus and Buffler, 1979).

Suicide clusters, suicide 'pacts,' copycat suicides, and other themes of suicide that include interpersonal associations between the living and the deceased are major concerns of indigenous suicide studies and prevention efforts. Youth may promise or make a silent 'pact' to attempt suicide in the event that a friend or family member attempts or completes suicide, or imitate that person in an effort to remain emotionally connected or loyal (Walls, Hautala, and Hurley, 2014: 53; MacNeil, 2008: 8). The urge to imitate suicide, displayed by pacts, clusters, and perhaps the high rate of suicide in indigenous populations more generally, may be grounded in a 'self-destructive identity' created and perpetuated by media and other communication outlets. Returning to Niezen's (2015) analysis of Tarde elaborates this point:

> Tarde's emphasis on the social significance of communication media points to one of the ways that ideas can influence the shaping of identity, sometimes resulting in collective acceptance of self-destruction as part of the nature of one's being. Media coverage that portrays the youth of a particular community as self-destructive and without hope can indirectly reinforce self-stereotyping in that direction. The scripts for possible lives communicated by media can directly and indirectly include the purposeful end of one's life. Representations of a community in crisis, suffering not only from the immediate effects of suicide, but in the simplest explanation conveyed to the public consumers of suffering, committing suicide in response to high levels of poor health, addictions, family violence, poverty, and unemployment, can indirectly add force to ideas about how one is expected to suffer and act upon a condition of suffering. Popular depictions and explanations of suicide risk reinforcing preexisting stereotypes of aboriginal social pathology and behavioral irresponsibility, solidifying the place of self-destruction in the feedback loop of personal identity.
>
> (2015: 109)

A 'self-destructive identity' may represent both process and product of the symbolic violence surrounding youth. Consistently framed as 'at risk' for suicide, substance abuse, behavioral disorders, and other physical or mental health issues, indigenous youth may eventually embody the features commonly associated with being at risk, effectively adopting an 'at risk identity.' It is essential to understand to what extent the relationships between indigenous youth and surrounding social institutions and agents (i.e., school, teacher, judicial system, mental health organization, counselors, and media) include and exhibit symbolic violence, described by French Sociologist Pierre Bourdieu as

> that invisible power which can be exercised only with the complicity of those who do not want to know that they are subject to it or even that they themselves exercise it . . . the practical recognition through which the dominated, often unwittingly, contribute to their own domination by tacitly accepting, in advance, the limits imposed on them.
>
> (Bourdieu, 1995, quoted in Samuel, 2013: 169)

The role of identity in indigenous youth suicide leans heavily toward the topic of stigma—"the situation of the individual who is disqualified from full social acceptance" (Goffman, 1963)—and deservedly so. American Indian youth, for instance, may avoid or fail to seek mental health services due to the fear of judgement and ostracism by the community (Freedenthal and Stiffman, 2007), and the stigma surrounding mental illness may prevent timely intervention (Grandbois, 2005). Further exacerbating the mental health status of American Indians is the double stigma of being "crazy" (Ibid.) and a member of a discriminated ethnic group (Gary, 2005). Exploring the roles that identity and image play in youth suicide, however, requires study of the symbolic and structural violence circulating in and around Tribal societies.

Recent research on the influence of stereotype and stigma on indigenous health disparities in general, in perhaps an unintended sense, already point to symbolic violence as a powerful force in indigenous health disparities. Grandbois and Sanders' (2012) study of the health effects of stereotype on American Indian elders, for example, emphasizes the "cultural genocide" and historical trauma resulting "from colonialism, acculturative stress, cultural bereavement, genocide, and racism that has been *generalized, internalized, and institutionalized*" (389: italics added). The process of "self-invalidation, where characteristics of the invalidating environment are internalized as a negative self-description" leads to "a tendency to invalidate affective experiences, to look to others for accurate reflections of external reality, and to oversimplify the ease of solving life's problems (Linehan, 1993)" (Ibid. 390). Shifting back to indigenous youth suicide specifically, MacNeil emphasizes "racial stereotypes that portray the aboriginal as inferior shape their consciousness and undermine their self-worth" (2008: 7).

The impact that stigma, stereotype, and other forces of structural and symbolic violence circulating in and around indigenous communities may have on youth suicide, however, remains an open question. Answering such a question requires researchers to be in indigenous communities, conversing with Tribal and non-Tribal members and observing daily interactions and use of symbols. As stated previously, effective research on indigenous youth suicide is incumbent on deeper knowledge of the Tribal communities and the everyday contexts in which youth suicide occurs. Unfortunately, the ethnographic approach, designed to map out the cultural terrain of ethnic groups, is perhaps the most underrepresented approach utilized in indigenous youth suicide. In her critical review of the literature on American Indian youth suicide, Strickland (1996) argued persistently for increased participant observation, the core method of ethnographic research, as well as participatory action research, grounded theory, historical case study, and descriptive analysis as methods capable of pushing the youth suicide research agenda.

Critique of Social Science Approaches to Youth Suicide

In this review of the literature, works that include overtly prevention-intervention as an end goal for research fall within the minority. Regardless of the methods used (qualitative, quantitative, or mixed methods), failing to consider potential applications of research for suicide prevention, especially in the initial phases of research design, is a glaring issue in indigenous youth suicide research—an issue potentially influenced by motivations for academic research. Researchers must ask the question: Is our search for applicable answers to indigenous youth suicide affected by competing motivations—personal, professional, and ideologically based motivations—that reduce the potential impact of social science research on youth suicide prevention? It is essential to turn the lens of anthropology inward and analyze the values-based motivations for research and treatment of health disparities—an approach described by medical anthropologists Lock and Scheper-Hughes as the "critical interpretive approach." The critical interpretive approach is understood and utilized in this book as the act of addressing "the moral, political and ideological value commitments underlying the choices made by those in control of the research [and treatment] process" (1990; brackets inserted).

Mackin, Perkins, and Furrer (2012), highlighting one such value commitment, critique the choice that many social scientists make when placing the "academic debate in the literature" above conducting research that is immediately applicable to prevention efforts and representative of Tribal views, needs, concerns, and real-life needs of youth:

> distinct disconnect between research and the ability to effectively communicate knowledge gained through research to staff, especially non-clinical staff, working directly with AI/AN youth in complex socioeconomic environments. This gap may be due at least partially to the (understandable) tendency of researchers to design their studies with an eye to academic debates in the existing literature, rather than to what questions might best be translated into actionable information for practitioners. However, two perspectives need not be mutually exclusive.
>
> (21)

Reviews of prevention-intervention programs and efforts in indigenous communities clearly display the benefits of coupling mental health and public health initiatives with research and data collection. Simultaneously, literature on prevention-intervention highlights the efficacy of specific prevention practices while critically analyzing the value of the research that informs practice. Literature reviews of mental health policy and suicide prevention-intervention address the need to recognize underlying causes for suicidal ideation, a demand for culturally sensitive treatment models, the over-reliance on a Western medical model versus supporting and integrating traditional indigenous medical models, and the need to question evidence-based practices, which are favored over exploring 'practice-based evidence.' Specifically addressing the Western medical model, Goodkind et al. (2010) state:

> Our conclusions are that these [mental health program] resources should be predicated on an understanding that the western health care system should support the effective healing practices and teachings that already exist in Native American communities. Behavioral health care in Native communities should not be something that Native American cultural teachings and practices must get integrated into; on the contrary, to be effective, western behavioral health systems must find ways to support Native healing practices. When we address this sensitive issue, we cannot assume that all people share the same perspective. A very wide spectrum of beliefs among Native people, ranging from people who speak their Native language and follow traditional spiritual practices and values, to others who have a Native cultural identity but are Christian, to those who are fully immersed in the dominant culture and do not speak their native language or practice traditional religion exists. *It is important for providers and systems to be aware of this diversity of beliefs and practices and to avoid assumptions.*
>
> (6; italics added)

Echoing Goodkind et al. (2010), Sahota and Kastelic (2014) call for further collaboration between indigenous communities, researchers, and mental health workers, making "cultural modifications" to mental health programs, education of non-Tribal health workers, and more direct support for and inclusion of traditional spiritually driven health approaches. While the topic of 'true prevention' is not outright discussed in the literature on indigenous youth suicide and mental health, Sahota and Kastelic hit upon the topic of true prevention by emphasizing the underlying causes for suicide patterns:

> There are multiple angles from which suicide prevention could be approached. Dr. Alex Crosby (medical epidemiologist, Division of Violence Prevention, CDC) commented that addressing issues underlying suicide, such as violence and substance abuse, can enable tribes to make an impact on multiple health priorities at the same time. Communities might also consider strategically working on improving intermediate outcomes related to suicide prevention. Some of these could include screening and treatment rates of depression and substance abuse, according to Kimberly Ross-Toledo. Other intermediate outcomes could include pride in cultural identity and a stronger sense of community belonging.
>
> (91)

In an earlier publication, Sahota and Kastelic (2012) review the criteria of "evidence" within evidence-based treatment and practices. A consequence of granting agencies' preference for evidence-based treatment precludes Tribes' pursuit of grants and support. Tribes often require technical assistance to conduct evidence-based research, which effectively forces Tribes to choose between shouldering the cost of exploring different suicide surveillance and treatment options and accepting the stricter guidelines that may accompany funding and technical support provided by granting agencies. Developing evidence-based treatments may also require measurements and surveillance of traditional healing methods. Gaining measurable results may be complicated due to hesitation on behalf of Tribal peoples who value confidentiality during ceremony and mistrust Euro-American surveillance and authority.

A salient reason for being critical of evidence-based treatment, however, is an inherent exclusion of practice-based evidence. Practice-based evidence, as described by Sahota and Kastelic, is an approach that would "inductively develop evidence based on routine health care practices used on the ground, rather than deductively developing hypotheses and testing them in clinical trials" (108). At the same time, Sahota and Kastelic cite "organizations serving AI/AN communities [that] have also called for practice-based evidence, which uses real-life practice as a basis for building evidence, as an alternative to the evidence-based practice paradigm" (108).

Validation and replicability, goals of evidence-based research and treatment, may be incompatible with indigenous knowledge systems, perhaps leading researchers to deny or downplay the value of indigenous knowledge systems and treatment methods. On the other hand, practice-based evidence recognizes that indigenous health models and treatments are "culturally validated and culturally replicated"—as opposed to scientifically validated and replicated—within specific communities. In commonsense terms, culturally based methods of understanding and treatment developed through cultural institutions over long periods of time "work." Tribes may view (coerced) attempts to replicate evidence-based treatments from one indigenous community to another as infeasible and representative of continuing institutional racism:

> Today's Native communities should not be required to use interventions that may be ineffective for them just because those programs have been deemed evidence-based in other populations.
>
> (Ibid. 109; see also Allen et al., 2014)

Further, if AI/AN communities do attempt to adapt mainstream evidence-based interventions to make them more specific to local contexts and culture, they may not produce the same results as they do for other populations. Kimberly Ross-Toledo is the executive director for the Coalition for Healthy and Resilient Youth in New Mexico and was part of the Project TRUST partnership. She said,

> By requiring AI/AN communities to implement evidence-based programming and alter it for cultural relevancy, the fidelity may be compromised and so you won't see the same result as in other communities. Then it looks like you're not doing the work appropriately, which impacts funding. Evidence-based practice is another form of institutional racism—it's a policy and practice that sets us up to fail.
>
> (109–110)

In their list of policy recommendations, Project TRUST members call for a shift in emphasis and funding from evidence-based practice to practice-based evidence.

Analysis and Dissemination

This case study is a humble attempt at addressing gaps within the field of youth suicide research in indigenous communities, using mixed methods—largely qualitative—to capture the elusive meanings of youth suicide in an Ojibwa community. I rely on descriptive analysis and creative ethnographic writing to explore and highlight meanings of youth suicide and cultural concepts of death, life, health, and treatment. Creative ethnographic writing is also utilized to avoid the "distinct disconnect" that exists between researchers and Tribal communities. Descriptive analysis of interview materials and field notes places less emphasis on theoretical and methodological debates while re-centering analysis on lived experiences and perspectives, allowing both researcher and reader to interpret, in novel ways, the context of suicide (e.g., Matsuda, 2014).

This study does not include quantitative data collection, which I, as a qualitative researcher, am not qualified to undertake in any case. Available statistics from local, state, and national sources describing suicide risk factors, behavioral risk factors, protective factors, and mortality data are briefly analyzed in Chapter 2. Extensive statistical data on suicide in the Sault Tribe are sorely lacking, and available statistics rely on inadequate reporting procedures. Review of statistical methods and nuances of suicide reporting, rather, provide a basis for interview questions outlining suicide reporting procedures, data collection and analysis, involvement of social scientists in suicide studies, use of existing statistics (local, tribal, state, and national) to support prevention efforts, and attitudes and conditions within the community that impact accurate reporting of suicide in the Sault Tribe (stigma, views on suicide). Such questions highlight the limitations of current suicide reporting and data while also highlighting the need for qualitative methods and a critical-interpretive approach.

Grounded theory, in the most basic sense, became an unintentional component of data collection and analysis. Grounded theory, according to Pulla (2014), is an attempt at not being "constrained by literature when coding."

> Researchers clearly avail the opportunity not to impose concepts on the data and instead wait for those concepts to emerge from the data. In other words, the research does not begin with a theory, the theory is the outcome. It is a set of grounded concepts integrated around a central theme to form a theoretical framework that explains how and why persons, organizations, communities or nations experience and respond to events, challenges or problematic situations (Corbin and Holt, 2011).
>
> (Pulla, 2014: 15–16)

I am hesitant to claim grounded theory as an intentional component of the research framework. In the most basic sense, however, the grounded theory approach is present in this work in that (1) the framework, while informed by the literature, was not guided by any theoretical paradigm or methodological approach save basic ethnographic methods and descriptive analysis; (2) concepts of death, identity, health, and risk factors for suicide "emerge from data," as opposed to data aligning with established theoretical models and concepts related to the research topic; and (3) this "research does not begin with a theory," rather, any theory on indigenous youth suicide generated here "is the outcome" of concepts and themes that "emerge from the data" (Ibid.).

Ethnographic methods of data collection, specifically participant observation and interviews, complement descriptive analysis. Ethnographic methods allow for inclusion of Tribal history, multi-generational, family histories and significant events and eras, and the construction of a timeline for the phenomena of youth suicide. Using multiple lines of evidence also highlights suicide and mental health disparities as culminating events (e.g., Herring, 1994; Kraus and Buffler, 1979). Tribal and non-Tribal attitudes toward life, death, suicide, health, and identity (i.e., what it means to be an "at-risk youth" in the Sault Tribe?/What is an Indian?) expose the value motivations, as well as symbolic violence and structural violence operating in institutions serving and surrounding Tribal youth.

Standing at the fork between the well-traveled path of conventional scholarly writing and the more colorful trail of creative ethnographic writing, I chose the latter. Creative ethnographic writing, as a method of expressing research results through various literary styles (poetry, short story, creative writing), allows the reader (and writer) to become more empathetically attached to subject matter and the community. Exposure to the lived experience, the social, economic, and cultural realities of indigenous people, may stimulate critical, inclusive, and healing conversation on the topic of suicide. According to Gray et al. (2010):

> Creative expression and storytelling establish a nonthreatening environment where people can develop a sense of belonging, reflect on personal experience, and reconnect with tribal traditions. This personal empowerment may lead to changes in community norms that reaffirm the traditional values and beliefs that have maintained survival and resilience.
>
> (187–188)

Such attachments and expressions stem from a realization by anthropologists that "we hold in our hands real people's lives" (Waterston and Vesperi, 2009). As powerfully discussed by contributors to Waterson and Vesperi (2009), advocating for vulnerable members of society often requires researchers to step outside the bounds of academic language and conventional formats for dissemination of research and promote public engagement with the aim of social justice, as well as social science.

I was not alone on the path of creative ethnographic writing, however, and throughout the research process, from developing framework to writing style consulted and shared field notes, transcripts, and writing samples with community members, interview participants, and academic mentors. Poetry, creative nonfiction, and stand-alone extracts from interview transcripts and field notes punctuate this work, vividly displaying the social and physical landscape of Bowheting, and in raw, unguarded form the hopes, fears, and theories of Tribal and non-Tribal community members facing youth suicide. The result is, I believe, a complementary mixture of creative writing, use of academic literature, and descriptive analysis that meets the emotional-cultural needs of the Tribal community, as well as the standards of academia. At present, this study lacks the time and space needed to fully and holistically explore this topic, addressing the psychological, social, historical, and cultural aspects of youth suicide, as well as reliable quantitative data to complement the qualitative evidence presented. Creative writing, then, is used to fill the spaces in between the many unanswered questions facing the researcher, reader, and community while coloring the social, political, economic, historical, and environmental conditions responsible for inducing mental trauma and sense of despair (Jackson, 2010, 2011; Barker and Johnston, 2008).

I cannot help feeling that my pursuit of unconventional writing styles represents a choice between loyalty to the community with which I work and the academic community. As Walls, Hautala, and Hurley (2014) expressed, however, researchers must not discount Tribal members' all too often "silenced voices" within the research decisions and final published texts of ethnographic work on health disparities. Rather, researchers must treat indigenous stakeholders as partners in an open and frank discussion of ongoing and future research and treatment. Treating indigenous communities as partners also includes writing for, to, and with Tribal people (Atalay, 2012). In short, anthropologists are not ethically permitted to deny, "silence," or otherwise muffle the voices of the communities with which we work, especially when the community or topic at the center of our work includes vulnerable populations.

Hopefully, emphasizing Tribal reflections on youth suicide and the development of underlying conditions will redress the marginalization of indigenous health and treatment models. At the same time, replacing academic-convention scientific views with lived indigenous realities and creative-emotional language can allow researchers to reframe indigenous conspiratorial opinions regarding health disparities as valid theoretical explanations based on existing socio-environmental degradations and colonial contexts (Briggs, 2004).

Limitations

Time was a limiting factor in this study, restricting my ability to include and more thoroughly utilize a larger number of methodological and theoretical sources on suicide (indigenous or otherwise), as well as historical and cultural sources on the Ojibwa. As a result of the relatively small amount of data collected, this work is best characterized as a pilot study.

Yet, more analysis and discussion can be yielded from the interviews, field notes, and documentary sources than is presented here. That said, the largest limitation of this study may be the author's ability and resources to fully explore the data. This limitation partially motivated the decision to include long excerpts from transcripts and field notes, which are valuable to community members, researchers, and policymakers as points of independent analysis and discussion. Few reliable quantitative sources exist in this community regarding youth suicide with which to compare.

During earlier communications, the Sault Tribe Board of Directors voiced its concern over including minors in this study. Both the researcher and the Tribal Board of Directors agreed that while youth could be included in future studies, the current study would include only adults. Recruiting interview participants from administrative fields, whose responsibilities already included describing programming and policies related to youth suicide, also served to meet many Tribal concerns over protection of community members while providing an essential overview of youth suicide and mental health from an administrative perspective. As a result, however, youth and everyday community members were not actively included in the structured interview portion of this study, and their perspectives remain to be heard. The lack of direct injection of young voices - the concerns, viewpoints, experiences and generational stances toward youth suicide, mental health and contributing factors - is perhaps the most regrettable limitation of this work. In the words of a Sault Tribe mental health administrator who recognizes and advocates for inclusion of youth within surveys of health and wellbeing amongst youth,

> teens tell us we don't understand them all the time. In our survey, they said you don't understand us, you know, and you have to ask us. So I think understanding teens and peer groups and peer pressure and all that stuff . . . more information in those areas would be very helpful.
>
> (C1371615)

The majority of field work and interviews were conducted in the Sault Sainte Marie and Sugar Island area. While a large number of Sault Tribe members live in and around Sault Sainte Marie and Sugar Island, many Tribal members live in outlying counties within the Seven County Service Area, throughout the State of Michigan, and beyond. Since Sault Sainte Marie is one of the very few "urban" areas in the Upper Peninsula, restricted focus on this area excludes areas that are more rural.

The literature on youth suicide in indigenous communities and health disparities in indigenous populations continues to expand. The growth of this literature is a positive sign in that the research community and agencies responsible for responding to health disparities, both pushed by public recognition and media recognition of this issue, are seeking answers to the dilemma of indigenous youth suicide. The overall number and rate of publications to date make a more thorough analysis of the literature beyond what is presented here impossible within the scope of this work. Hopefully, the theme of the literature review (which is largely critical-interpretive) and themes of this work (ethnomedical, collaborative based, emic, emancipatory) will feed into existing gaps in the literature and health policy, to inform, alongside the developing literature, current and future researchers and health care professionals. As discussed in this section, a further reason for showing preference to historical, cultural, or mental health literature specifically related to the Anishnaabek, if not the Bowheting Ojibwa, is the overgeneralization which occurs (and continues to occur) in the field of indigenous health research.

Human Subjects Institutional Review Board (HSIRB) Approval, Tribal Review and Approval

Western Michigan University provided Human Subjects Institutional Review Board Approval for this case study. After providing the Sault Tribe with both the Western Michigan University HSIRB and an oral presentation and question-and-answer session on June 13, 2015, the Sault Sainte Marie Tribe of Chippewa Indians Board of Directors and Chairman approved of the research in support of a master's thesis by referendum, with a vote of 12 for and zero against (see Appendix C). The fact that the community included in this case study is named within the resulting book is somewhat unorthodox, especially given the sensitive nature of the research topic. Previous versions of book chapters and creative pieces have been published in the Sault Tribe Newspaper, *Win Awenen Nisitotung*, and the author presented early in a public forum. The community, aware and supportive of research, after consistent questioning from the author in informal circles and in interviews, agreed that the research results should be published openly for the community to view and discuss while including the name of the community.

Conclusion

It is my hope that the knowledge and understanding gained through this study of youth suicide in an Ojibwa community will lead this community to address and reconcile a history and culture that is as beautiful as it is conflicted. The Anishnaabek understand the world through stories laden with meanings. Passed around the fire in the cold winter, from generation to generation, our stories were told in small parts. Each story, no matter how large or small, is woven into the larger tapestry of the human history. Like a stream feeding into a river, and that river flowing into a larger body of water, all of our lives and our stories feed into each other.

Stories hold special meanings, each varying from person to person, place to place, and culture to culture. True meanings come to the surface in their own time. The story one hears as a child will have great import in adulthood, and the adult will add his or her experiences to that story. In this way, stories are more complete, helpful, and hopeful for the next generation. The story I am about to tell is not complete, and builds upon previous stories told by and about the Bowheting Ojibwa, and indigenous people of North America in general. Youth suicide is a story of many meanings—identity, purpose, stigma, colonialism, history, historical trauma, resilience, as well as other meanings the reader will take from this work. Youth suicide in indigenous communities is a story of hope versus hopelessness.

Works Cited

Allen, J., Mohatt, G. V., Beehler, S., and Rowe, H. L. (2014) "People Awakening: Collaborative Research to Develop Cultural Strategies for Prevention in Community Intervention." *American Journal of Community Psychology*. 54 (1), 100–111.

Atalay, S. (2012) *Community Based Archaeology: Research With, by and for Indigenous and Local Communities*. Berkeley: University of California Press.

Barber, R. J., and Berdan, F. F. (1998) "The Scope of Ethnohistory." In *The Emperor's Mirror: Understanding Cultures Through Primary Sources*. Tucson: University of Arizona Press, 5–32.

Barker, H. M., and Johnston, B. R. (2008) *The Consequential Damages of Nuclear War: The Rongelap Report*. Walnut Creek, CA: Left Coast Press.

Barlow, A., Tingey, L., Cwik, M., Goklish, N., Larzelere-Hinton, F., Lee, A., Suttle, R., Mullany, B., and Walkup, J. (2012) "Understanding the Relationship Between Substance Use and Self-Injury in American Indian Youth." *The American Journal of Drug and Alcohol Abuse*. 38 (5), 403.

Beck, Aaron T., Brown, Gary, & Steer, Robert A. (1989). Prediction of eventual suicide in psychiatric inpatients by clinical ratings of hopelessness. *Journal of Consulting and Clinical Psychology*, 57(2), 309.

Briggs, C. (2004) "Theorizing Modernity Conspiratorially: Science, Scale, and the Political Economy of Public Discourse in Explanations of a Cholera Epidemic." *American Ethnologist*. 31 (2), 164–187.

Centers for Disease Control (CDC) (2009) "Suicide: Facts at a Glance." www.cdc.gov/violenceprevention/pdf/suicide-datasheet-a.pdf

Cleland, Charles E. (1992) *Rites of Conquest: The History and Culture of Michigan's Native Americans*. University of Michigan Press.

Cleland, Charles E. (2001) *The Place of the Pike (Gnoozhekaaning): A History of the Bay Mills Indian Community*. University of Michigan Press.

Doll, J., and Brady, K. (2013) "Project HOPE: Implementing Sensory Experiences for Suicide Prevention in a Native American Community." *Occupational Therapy in Mental Health*. 29 (2), 149–158.

Durkheim, E. (1951) *Suicide: A Study in Sociology*. Translated by J. A. Spaulding and G. Simpson, edited with Introduction by G. Simpson. Glencoe, IL: Free Press.

Edmonson, J., and Kitchens, J. (2000) *Hopelessness, Self-Efficacy, Self-Esteem and Powerlessness in Relation to American Indian Suicide*. University of North Texas; Proquest Dissertations.

Fadiman, A. (2012) *The Spirit Catches You and You Fall Down: A Hmong Child, Her American Doctors, and the Collison of Two Cultures*. New York: Farrar, Straus & Giroux.

Farmer, P., Nizeye, B., Stulac, S., and Keshavjee, S. (2006). Structural Violence and Clinical Medicine (Policy Forum). *PLoS Medicine*, 3(10), E449.

Freedenthal, S., and Stiffman, A. (2007) "'They Might Think I Was Crazy': Young American Indians' Reasons for Not Seeking Help When Suicidal." *Journal of Adolescent Research*. 22 (1), 58–77.

Gary, F. A. (2005) "Stigma: Barrier to Mental Health Care Among Ethnic Minorities." *Issues in Mental Health Nursing*. 26 (10), 979–999.

Goffman, E. (1963). *Stigma: Notes on the management of spoiled identity*. Prentice Hall.

Goodkind, J., Gorman, B., Hess, J., Parker, D., and Hough, R. (2015) "Reconsidering Culturally Competent Approaches to American Indian Healing and Well-Being." *Qualitative Health Research*. 25 (4), 486–499.

Goodkind, J., Ross-Toledo, R., John, K., Hall, S., Ross, J., Freeland, L., Coletta, L., Becenti-Fundark, L., Poola, E., Begay-Roanhorse, T., and Lee, C. (2010) "Promoting Healing and Restoring Trust: Policy Recommendations for Improving Behavioral Health Care for American Indian/Alaska Native Adolescents." *American Journal of Community Psychology*. 46 (3), 386–394.

Gough, K. (1968) "Anthropology and Imperialism." *Monthly Review*. 19 (11), 12–27.

Grandbois, D. (2005) "Stigma of Mental Illness Among American Indian and Alaska Native Nations: Historical and Contemporary Perspectives." *Issues in Mental Health Nursing*. 26 (10), 1001–1024.

Grandbois, D and Sanders, G. "Resilience and Stereotyping: The Experiences of Native American Elders." *Journal of Transcultural Nursing*. 23 (4) 389– 396.

Gray, N., Ore, B., Farnsworth, A., and Wolf, D. (2010) "Integration of Creative Expression into Community-Based Participatory Research and Health Promotion with Native Americans." *Fam Community Health*. 33 (3) 186–192.

Grewal, P., and Porter, J. (2007) "Hope Theory: A Framework for Understanding Suicidal Action." *Death Studies*. 31 (2), 131–154.

Health Canada (2013) "Facts on Suicide Rates." www.hc-sc.gc.ca/fniah-spnia/promotion/suicide/index-eng.php

Herne, M., Bartholomew, M., and Weahkee, R. (2014). Suicide Mortality Among American Indians and Alaska Natives, 1999–2009. *American Journal of Public Health, 104*(3), S336–342.

Herring, R. (1994) "Substance Use Among Native American Indian Youth: A Selected Review of Causality." *Journal of Counseling and Development*. 72 (6), 578–584.

Howard, M., and Millard, A. V. (1997) *Hunger and Shame: Child Malnutrition and Poverty on Mount Kilimanjaro*. New York and London: Routledge.

Hurston, Z. N. (1978) *Mules and Men* (Reprint, 1935) (Preface by F. Boas; introduction by R. E. Hemenway). Bloomington: Indiana University Press.

Jackson, D. (2010) "Shelter in Place: A First Nation Community in Canada's Chemical Valley." *Interdisciplinary Environmental Review*. 11 (4), 249–262.

Jackson, D. (2011) "Scents of Place: The Displacement of a First Nations Community in Canada." *American Anthropologists*. 113 (4), 606–618.

Jackson, D. (2002). *Our elders lived it: American Indian identity in the city*. DeKalb, Ill: Northern Illinois University Press.

Jackson, D., and Chapleski, E. (2000) "Not Traditional, Not Assimilated: Elderly American Indians and the Notion of 'Cohort.'" *Journal of Cross-Cultural Gerontology*. 15 (3), 229–259.

Kleinman, A. (1978) "Concepts and a Model for the Comparison of Medical Systems as Cultural Systems." *Social Science and Medicine*. Part B Medical Anthropology. (12), 85–93.

Kovacs, M., Beck, A., and Weissman, A. (1975) "Hopelessness." *Suicide and Life- Threatening Behavior*. 5 (2), 98–103.

Kral, M., Links, P., and Bergmans, Y. (2012) "Suicide Studies and the Need for Mixed Methods Research." *Journal of Mixed Methods Research*. 6 (3), 236–249.

Kraus, R., and Buffler, F. (1979) "Sociocultural Stress and the American Native in Alaska: An Analysis of Changing Patterns of Psychiatric Illness and Alcohol Abuse Among Alaska Natives." *Culture, Medicine and Psychiatry*. 3 (2), 111–151.

Lock, M. (2002) *Twice Dead: Organ Transplants and the Reinvention of Death*. Berkley: University of California.

Lock, M., and Scheper-Hughes, N. (1990) "A Self-Critical Approach to Medical Anthropology." In *Medical Anthropology: Contemporary Theory and Method*. Edited by T. M. Johnson and C. F. Sargent. New York: Praeger.

Mackin, J., Perkins, T., and Furrer, C. (2012) "The Power of Protection: A Population Based Comparison of Native and Non-Native Youth Suicide Attempters." *American Indian and Alaska Native Mental Health Research* (Online). 19 (2), 20–54.

MacNeil, M. (2008) "An Epidemiologic Study of Aboriginal Adolescent Risk in Canada: The Meaning of Suicide." *Journal of Child and Adolescent Psychiatric Nursing*. 21 (2), 3–12.

Matsuda, D. (2010) "A Study of Army Suicides in Iraq; a 2010 Study in 2014 Context" (rev. 2010) "Cultural Knowledge and Analysis Paper: Towards a Holistic, Life History Study of Army Suicide (unclassified)." United States Army, Cultural Advisor Services.

May, P. and Dizmang, L. (1974) "Suicide and the American Indian." *Psychiatric Annals*. 4 (11), 22–23, 27–28.

Mcgregor, L, Gzik, D, Manitowabi, D, Maar, M, and Corbiere, C. (2011). Serious Complications for Patients, Care Providers and Policy Makers: Tackling the Structural Violence of First Nations People Living with Diabetes in Canada. *International Indigenous Policy Journal, 2*(1).

McIntosh, J. L., and Santos, J. F. (1980) "Suicide Among Native Americans: A Compilation of Findings." *Omega: Journal of Death and Dying*. 11 (4), 303–316.

Niezen, R. (2015) "The Durkheim-Tarde Debate and the Social Study of Aboriginal Youth Suicide." *Transcultural Psychiatry*. 52 (1), 96–114.

Olson, L. and Wahab, S. (2006) "American Indians and Suicide: A Neglected Area of Research." *Trauma, Violence & Abuse.* 7 (1) 19–33.

Pettingell, S, Bearinger, L, Skay, C, Resnick, M, Potthoff, S, and Eichhorn, J. (2008). Protecting Urban American Indian Young People from Suicide. American Journal of Health Behavior, 32 (5), 465–476.

Pulla, V. (2014) "Grounded Theory Approach in Social Research." *Space and Culture, India.* 2 (3), 14–23.

Sahota, P. C., and Kastelic, S. (2012) "Culturally Appropriate Evaluation of Tribally Based Suicide Prevention Programs: A Review of Current Approaches." *Wicazo Sa Review.* 27 (2), 99–127.

Sahota, P. C., and Kastelic, S. (2014) "Tribally Based Suicide Prevention Programs: A Review of Current Approaches." *Wicazo Sa Review.* 29 (1), 77.

Samuel, C. (2013) "Symbolic Violence and Collective Identity: Pierre Bourdieu and the Ethics of Resistance." *Social Movement Studies*, 1–17.

Shaughnessy, L., Doshi, S. R., and Jones, S. E. (2004) "Attempted Suicide and Associated Health Risk Behaviors among Native American High School Students." *Journal of School Health.* 74 (5), 177.

Shore, J. (1975) "Abstracts and Reviews: American Indian Suicide: Fact and Fantasy." *Psychiatry.* 38 (1), 86–91.

Sontag, S. (1978) *Illness as Metaphor.* New York: Farrar, Straus and Giroux.

Starn, O. (2011) "Here Come the Anthros Gain: The Strange Marriage of Anthropology and Native America." *Cultural Anthropology.* 26 (2), 179–204.

Stewart, S., Sherry, S., Comeau, M., Mushquash, C., Collins, P., and Van Wilgenburg, H. (2011) "Hopelessness and Excessive Drinking Among Aboriginal Adolescents: The Mediating Roles of Depressive Symptoms and Drinking to Cope." *Depression Research and Treatment.* (2011)

Straight, B., Pike, I., Hilton, C., and Oesterle, M. (2015) "Suicide in Three East African Pastoralist Communities and the Role of Researcher Outsiders for Positive Transformation: A Case Study." *Culture, Medicine, and Psychiatry.* 39 (3), 557–578.

Strickland, C. J. (1996) "Suicide Among American Indian, Alaskan Native, and Canadian Aboriginal Youth: Advancing the Research Agenda." *International Journal of Mental Health.* 25 (4), 11–32.

Tingey, L., Cwik, M. F., Goklish, N., Larzelere-Hinton, F., Lee, A., Suttle, R., Walkup, J. T., and Barlow, A. (2014) "Risk Pathways for Suicide Among Native American Adolescents." *Qualitative Health Research.* 24 (11), 1518–1526.

Trouillot, M-R. (1997) *Silencing the Past: Power and Production of History.* Boston, MA: Beacon Press.

Walls, M., Hautala, D., and Hurley, J. (2014) "'Rebuilding Our Community': Hearing Silenced Voices on Aboriginal Youth Suicide." *Transcultural Psychiatry.* 51 (1), 47–72.

Waterson, A. and Vesperi, M. (2009) *Anthropology Off the Shelf: Anthropologists on Writing.* Malden, MA: Blackwell.

"The wind is perfect," says my older brother as he exhales another noxious cloud of smoke.

"I know," I say, weaving in and out of the blue-gray tendrils. The Western sky, with its radiant red, gold, and purple streams of light slowly, but surely, submits to the dark blue and the ranks of stars marching from the east.

A maroon pickup rumbles up the road and turns into the short driveway. Our cousin CJ, wearing a flannel jacket, work boots, and blue jeans (the official uniform of Northern Michiganders), hops out and meets us on the concrete pad porch. "You guys ready?"

"Yep," says Matt. "Got the lantern?"

"Yep. Just gotta be careful with the mantles. We only have three," he says, referring to the small bags that operate as cloth lightbulbs inside the gas lantern.

We top off a couple thermoses with strong, fresh coffee, jump into Matt's white Ford pickup, and head down the residential side streets of the Soo. In a few minutes, we hook a right and drive down Portage Avenue, which runs along the bank of the Saint Marys River on the American side.

"Better speed it up if we are going to make the eight o'clock boat, Matty," says CJ.

Matt glances at the dash clock. It reads 7:57 p.m.

"We should make it," he says. The truck lurches forward as he pushes the pedal a bit—just in case.

We turn into the ferry docking area on the left and see that the red and white craft is still moored to the mainland dock and loading a line of vehicles. Every year the price for transit seems to jump a buck or two. Since it is cheaper to cross as a pedestrian than as a vehicle passenger, we would normally avoid the higher price by slipping out of the truck, walking on the ferry and walking off the boat on the other side. Unfortunately, CJ and I didn't have the opportunity. Well, that and I did not feel like following CJ's suggestion and executing a "ninja roll" from a moving vehicle.

The station wagon in front of us clears the rusty on-ramp. Matt drives slowly over the steel grating toward the ramp, and the Ford heaves as we roll up and onto the metal deck. As our back tires clear the ramp, the deck worker, who guides vehicles on and off the ship and collects fares, holds up four fingers. As directed, we make roll between the yellow lines marked "Lane 4."

Three more cars make it on after us. A dozen or so cars and trucks fill the ferry to half capacity. We shut down the engine and I jump out to escape further smoke inhalation. Raised in a family of smokers, it's a miracle I don't have lung cancer. I wander to the side railing of the one hundred and fifty foot long, rectangle shaped craft. A couple seconds later the truck doors slam and my cousin and brother walk up to either side and lean against the rail.

"Ready to murder some fish?" I say, looking up at my taller cousin.

CJ gives a stoic nod, and keeps up his intense stare across the water. To others it might seem a bit intimidating, but CJ's eyes always had a bit of a piercing glare in them. In fact, most of us seem to have that stoicness in the face. So much so that sometimes, even to our ignorance, we can seem intimidating or pissed. This has led to more than a few 'are you okay's.'

The ferry revs its engine, creating a high pitched whine, in preparation for the transit. The deckman casts the mooring lines and with a blow of the foghorn, we lurch out into the river. Immediately, the boat begins to turn up stream, beginning its dance with the current as we cross the five hundred-some yards between the mainland and Sugar Island.

Still a quarter mile distant, the island's dark green, ominous shading always reminds me of a story my grandmother told me about her brother, who fought as a Marine in the Pacific island-hopping campaigns of World War II. When he returned, one of the first places he stayed was on Sugar Island. She said it was never a good idea for him, after having fought on dark jungle islands, to then return home and stay on another island thick with brush and vegetation. I can see how, at night, Sugar Island can resemble the jungles of the South Pacific. He slept with a pistol under his pillow for years, she said.

To the first-time passenger the river-crossing process might seem crazy. Negotiating the strong currents requires the boat to turn ninety degrees upstream and sort of 'scoot' sideways, before righting itself just past midstream and slipping into the opposite docking station. Many times, it has seemed impossible that the pilot will fit the craft into the docking area before banging into the log pylons standing sentry on either side of the loading ramp. The dents in the steel railing and scrapes on the hull plenty testify to the difficulties of parking the unwieldy ship. Today, we are delivered safely to the other side.

The deckman lazily loops the lines over the mooring post as we jump back into the truck and turn the engine on. At his signal, we roll forward, exchange waves, and have-a-good-ones and bounce down the ramp and onto the ferry road. It's getting even darker and we need to hurry to use the last bit of daylight to prepare the boat, spear, and oars. The pickup speeds along the ferry road, which rises about twenty feet of shallow water on both sides, for two miles. Cool, late summer wind whips through the open windows. We hang a left on Shoreline drive and follow another two miles of twisty roads until we arrive at Uncle Mike's house and our launching point.

The two track driveway is dominated by saplings and brush, giving it the appearance of a dark green tunnel. When I was a kid, our families camped in the open, lightly forested area at head of the driveway during impromptu summertime gatherings. At night, we ran back and forth between the safety and warmth of a fire near the riverbank, and the fire and tents at the campground. We warded off the looming beasts of the enchanted forest tunnel with flashlights and hastily sought out staves in our continual quests for the sacred s'more. Twenty years later, we rumble down the same two-track on another nocturnal quest. My mind returns to childhood memories, and I wonder about beasts that replaced childhood imaginings and now stand at the edges of my adult fears. Matt reels me back in from my metaphysical wanderings when he throws the truck into park near one of several pole barns on the property . . .

The office phone interrupts our meeting with an obnoxious warbling cry. He cranes his head back and to the left to check the caller ID.

"If you get any calls you have to answer you can forget me, okay?"

"No, that's ok."

"I'll wait," I say, reaching forward toward the voice recorder that lies on the desk between us—with the same conviction as a person who doesn't want to pay the dinner tab reaching politely (and slowly) for his wallet.

"No, that's okay. They'll wait. That's part of being in charge."

"Perks of the job, eh?"

"Yeah," he says with a chuckle.

He looks tired. Too much sun this weekend? I wonder. Telling by the neat, raccoon pattern of white and red skin around his eyes, it could be the case. With summer in the UP only two months or less out of the year, who could blame him? People all around the Soo share his sentiment. Residents sit lazily in lawn chairs and cruise town with the windows down, soaking in every ray of sun before brutal cold forces them indoors and back to the vampiric lifestyle of the winter season.

He continues his description of how, from his knowledge, the community responds to death. Over the years, he experienced the loss of students to car accidents and sickness. One student lost his life in America's wars in the Middle East. He spoke of how proud he was of his students' reaction to the news, and their support for the fallen soldier's family.

"When the funeral service took place, 800 kids got the day off school. But none of them left. They all stayed behind to attend. It really restores the feeling as an administrator that kids know the right thing to do, no matter what. And his dad was very, very grateful for the way this community pulled together to honor his son."

Some students who passed on he had taught personally, though he recalls talking to all of the boys and girls who once walked the halls of the school. When the subject came to suicide, the atmosphere changed.

". . . You question the whole lotta why . . . You work really, really hard to help students. Help families. That's someone's little boy, that's someone's little girl who's the same age as my kids. And the unknown just happens. No matter what you do, the unknown is your biggest fear. And so you don't know what . . . there's no way to answer an unknown question. That is why I think we work so hard on [suicide] prevention, because at the end of the day all those other things we talked about, the scientific community can't answer. Even a car accident, which is so tragic, there are some definite answers to. But suicide is that great unknown where you don't . . . you just can't explain . . . I work at [xxxx] in the summertime. One of the kids that committed suicide was very good friends with one of the kids that worked there too, and this had been years ago. And they started memorial funds and all of those things. To

try and prevent this from ever happening again. And it's become their mission to help other people, which is a beautiful thing. But it doesn't answer the why."

The interview ends, and as I walk slowly to my truck in the school parking lot, I feel the "unknown" weighing heavily on me as well. I realize in moments like this, after another person pours his or her experiences and feelings out on the topic of tragic death, that my weight must pale in comparison to that felt by those who are closest to the very children most at risk for suicide. With every interview, I feel less like an anthropologist and more like a grief counselor. The passion with which the educators, clinic workers, traditional healers, social welfare workers, and various administrators in the Eastern Upper Peninsula serve Tribal and non-Tribal youth is clear—as is their concern over the unknowns of youth suicide. [PC1/072415]

2 Overview of Suicide in the Sault Tribe

It's always been [an issue]. . . . We didn't talk about it much as a kid, but it was always there. There was always somebody taking themselves out. And it's not just our young people anymore . . .

—Prayer Person, Tribal member, longtime resident of the EUP area [PC101/72415]

That's kind of a tough one to think back on. Because it's always been there, it just wasn't . . . I hate to use the word popular. But it came into focus more. And I can think back to even when I was in high school here or in college, it wasn't a topic to talk about. You didn't talk about it. You kind of brushed it under the carpet. In 2004 [that] was when it was really starting to be okay to talk about suicide. Because that's when the program started to identify these youth that needed the assistance, who needed the special care, who needed eyes on them all the time.

—Sault Area Schools Counselor, Tribal member, longtime resident of the EUP area [PC51/81215]

I've worked in education in this community for twenty years at Sault Schools. . . . I guess I wasn't well aware or we didn't necessarily sort out which were our Native kids, which ones weren't. We were a public school. That wasn't really on my radar. I think even then, though, we were dealing with kids—and again part of it is the economy, part of it is single family homes and a lot of risk factors—I can recall kids who were depressed and struggling or expressed some suicidal ideation. . . . As far as when did this become, start to become an issue? I can't think of any particular start date or turning point. I think it's been present and I think it's been an issue over time and probably fluctuates or varies depending on a variety of circumstances.

—Sault Area Schools Administrator, non-Tribal member, longtime resident of the EUP area [PC111/72215]

In 2011, the Michigan Department of Community Health reported that suicide was the leading cause of injury death in Michigan's Upper

Peninsula between 2007 and 2009 (State of Michigan, 2011). The Sault Tribe Alive Youth program, which operated from 2008 to 2012, cited within its federal grant application a 2006 rate of 17.4 suicides per 100,000 for all races in the Seven County Service Area (see Maps), a region that is home to the majority of Sault Tribe membership (Sault Tribe STAY Grant Appication, #1U79SM058400-01, 2008). During 2006 the national and state averages were 10.8 and 11.2 suicides per 100,000, respectively.

The active presence of the Upper Peninsula Suicide Prevention Coalition, the national Yellow Ribbon Campaign, and other grassroots suicide prevention and intervention programs indicate that Tribal and non-Tribal residents of Michigan's Eastern Upper Peninsula treat youth suicide as an existing threat requiring public attention and action. The above statistics and the development of prevention programs in and of themselves do not shed significant light on Native American suicide rates. Furthermore, existing records do not support public claims that suicide is a pervasive issue in the Sault Tribe community. Between 1970 and 2013, 12 percent of recorded suicides in Chippewa County, Michigan, which holds one of the largest populations of Native Americans, (predominantly Sault Tribe members), are American Indian and Alaska Native. With a total AI/AN population standing at nearly 16 percent of the total county population, Native Americans are underrepresented.[1] However, underrepresentation and otherwise inaccurate data on suicide attempts and completions is a common issue that is attributable to reliance on retrospective data, lack of common reporting procedures and standards, the inherent difficulties of examining suicide cases, and the potential for misclassifying or purposefully classifying apparent or potential suicides as other modes of death (MacNeil, 2008: 6).

The potential for misclassifications is evident in the frustrations of a Sault Tribal Heath Center administrator who has been working "for years to try and get data on birth rates, death rates." He points out that if a deceased person does not have a Tribal identification card on his or her person or the medical examiner does not receive notification of the person's Tribal membership, the death certificate may misrepresent the deceased's racial identity (Herne, Bartholomew, and Weahkee, 2014).

Even in the event the racial classification is accurately recorded, the nuances of the medical examination and reporting process itself may cause potential misrepresentation of manner of death. Unless a person leaves a suicide note, passes away as an obvious result of self-inflicted death, or leaves some other form of evidence that suicide may have played a role, a medical examiner cannot record the death as suicide. Suicide by drug overdose, for instance, cannot be recorded as suicide without existing proof that the overdose was intentional, such as a note or claims of suicide ideation by friends or family. Furthermore, in the event that self-inflicted injury or overdose with suicidal intentions does not immediately result in death, the eventual death may be recorded as accidental. As Chippewa County Medical Examiner Dr. Garlinghouse states, if "somebody succumbs to death after a suicide attempt and it's not immediate, it might not be called a suicide, whereas it really was. Were it not for the suicide attempt, they never would have had [an injury] and died."

Suicide may also carry with it a stigma, or a sense that the person and even the family and friends of an individual who completed suicide is viewed differently and perhaps negatively. A minority of interviewees (about 25 percent) respond to the question "What is suicide?" with "a selfish act" or similar opinions. Feeling that death by suicide is "selfish" or wrong could pressure family members to describe the death to authorities as accidental. In order to save a family from the pain and confusion that comes with suicide, medical doctors or county medical examiners responsible for filling out the official death certificates may lean away from suicide as cause of death.

A secondary effect of inaccurate data on indigenous suicide is the frustration of Tribal efforts at gaining funding and support for suicide prevention and intervention programs. For example, the inability to "show need," a major aspect of pursuing and receiving grant funding, in the form of accurate and persuasive statistical information reduced the Sault Tribe's chances for receiving recent grant funding and support, as described by a Sault Tribal Health Center administrator:

> We were working on a large grant through SAMSHA . . . so that we could bring services into our area to prevent youth suicide. One of the difficulties that we had was in presenting a need. And, you know, with grants you always have to present a need. The reason we had so much difficulty with it was because suicides are not maybe always reported consistently. How they're recorded can vary from county to county. That information is usually kept at the county coroner's office or the medical examiner, and tribes may or may not have access to that. Also, how does the death get reported? . . . It often comes down to how the information is kept. Is it difficult to access? And it's also difficult because you don't know if it's being recorded the same from one setting to the next. So, we ran into a lot of difficulty with that and I think there's a lot of room for research to be done here so that we can make more informed decisions. [PC7/120715]

Regardless of potential underrepresentation of Native Americans in the example of Chippewa County, state records display disparities in the age spectrum of suicide completions. Out of seventeen age brackets, (10–14, 15–19 . . . 85–89, 90+), suicides for "All Races" (minus AI/AN) occurred in all brackets except the youngest range, 10–14; and average age of suicide is 48.5–52.5. In comparison, AI/AN suicides occurred in the eight youngest age brackets (10–14 . . . 45–49), and average age of suicide is 28.75–32.75. Males were six and four times more likely to complete suicide in both groups, respectively (State of Michigan, Office of Vital Statistics, Accessed 2015).

Public Awareness and Discussion of Suicide

While media coverage may present indigenous youth suicide as an issue rising out of the 1990s and 2000s (e.g., Guerra, 2014; Dunphy, 1993; Almendrala, 2015; Horwitz, 2014), educators, mental health professionals, traditional healers, social workers, and administrators interviewed believe that suicide has been a serious issue for years, perhaps decades, before coming to light in the public and media. Recent trends in social media, a push for public education and increased awareness of suicide opened the way to discussions of suicide and mental health in American and Canadian communities. As stated by a suicide prevention committee member, local suicide prevention programs realized that "dispelling the myths that surround" suicide is a major aspect of prevention. One myth in particular is that "you don't talk about suicide because you give kids the idea to complete suicide, which isn't true. Talking about suicide doesn't cause suicide." [PC51/081215]

"I think that Facebook opened up the conversation," says a former Tribal juvenile probation officer, "because kids don't talk to people. We have the Yellow Ribbon [Campaign] on Facebook. We have the coalition for suicide prevention on there. We get a lot of communication that way from kids. They'll find information and then they'll contact people." [PC5/081215] Receiving a 'green light' from society to discuss mental health issues and suicidal ideation is also catalyzing youth to explore resources and self-advocate.

In a specific case described by a Sault Area Schools administrator, a middle school student experiencing a stressful home life "was able to identify that he was feeling depressed . . . was able to put it in words [and] have a conversation with staff members, so we were really able to intervene." "It was cute," she says, "with the technology now, the kid was actually kind of Googling some of the symptoms and emailed that information to a teacher he felt comfortable with." [PC111/072215] Interviewees often describe the internet as a site for bullying and hurtful statements ("just go kill yourself; get it over with") or a place for teens to plaster personal messages in the hopes of gaining attention. In this case, however, the internet provided an avenue for self-awareness and communication of mental health status, allowing a child to pursue a more open, healthier conversation on mental health.

Oral History of Suicide

With vacant suicide data before the 1970s and data which are, at best, generally reliable after the 1970s, it is difficult to explore when and to what extent suicide became an issue for Sault Tribe members. At this point, exploration of the prevalence or regularity of suicide and suicide ideation, as well as the presence and nature of risk factors through oral history, becomes essential. While examining the risk and protective factors of suicide is an established route of investigation, the role of social and cultural attitudes toward suicide (i.e., Taboo, rephrased here as the social acceptability or unacceptability of suicide as a form of death), as well as official nuances of suicide reporting remain outside of the typical research focus (Straight et al, 2015). Adding context to taboos related to suicide, however, requires an understanding of community responses to and beliefs regarding suicide, death, tragic death, and death as a biological, social, and metaphysical (spiritual) process.

Turning to multigenerational sources provides a degree of understanding of the historical development of suicide, suicide ideation and conditions contributing to suicide, and changes in attitudes toward suicide, death, and forms of tragic death. Elders, in this case, become sources of oral history, or recollections of the past that are not primarily handed down through a written record but are passed on by word of mouth from generation to generation. Oral histories and traditions constitute a people's ethnic history, often formed as stories, ceremonies, and cultural attachments to significant landmarks (Basso, 1996). Oral histories and traditions do more than provide a spoken history or set of memories—oral histories and traditions instill a sense of common values and identity. Discussing the topic of suicide and the factors that contributed to suicide with adults and elders may provide a clearer picture of the youth suicide trend as a social event.

If you ask an elder about the most challenging aspects of their childhood, they might try to sell you on a tall tale, describing in stone cold seriousness wrestling bears on the way to school or riding across the river on the backs of sturgeon. If you were sincere and patient and had a sense of humor, descriptions of poverty and discrimination, the effects of alcoholism, struggles to practice Ojibwa ceremonies and spirituality, or the destructive boarding school programs may cross their lips. Elders consider the state- and church-run boarding schools, which forced Indian children to replace traditional ways of life with Euro-American values and language—essentially ripping away one identity and replacing it with another—as especially harmful to indigenous families (e.g., Brown, 1970; Trafzer, Keller, and Sisquoc, 2006). Years after the boarding school period, however, elders continue to head cultural events and gatherings, promoting an ethnic identity and language that invited discrimination, displaying a strong sense of resilience and appreciation for cultural continuity.

Elders between 60 and 80 years of age, the then-children of mid-twentieth-century Bowheting, generally do not describe suicide as a regular issue in their youth. Sharing a seat with me and a woman elder at the Sugar Island Pow-Wow, for example, Brother John Haskell explained that "we never talked about those kinds of things," such as suicide in a "negative way—we always talked about health and things like that in a positive way." An elder in his mid-70s recalled, "Suicide didn't really happen. I can only remember one person [when I was young] who did it." [FN20/071915]

The presence of the Catholic Church, which enjoys a strong historical foothold in the Sault Sainte Marie area since the Jesuit-mission era of the seventeenth-century, and several other Christian denominations (Methodist, Lutheran, and Pentecostal) lends the possibility that reactions to suicide are muted within family and community circles due to Christian beliefs regarding suicide as a punishable act. Asked whether suicide was misreported or not discussed due to fear of religious taboo, however, the male elder quoted above simply but assertively replied, "no"—and if such a significant event did happen, he would have heard it as news of the event filtered through the small and close-knit community of Sugar Island and the surrounding area.

In the 1930s, a time when many current Sault Tribe elders (aged 70 or above) were in their youth, anthropologist Mary Hilger (1951) reported in her study amongst nine Ojibwa communities in Minnesota, Wisconsin, and Michigan that "[s]uicide occurs today, but none of the [elders] recalled ever having heard of it in the early days." She goes on to quote a fellow researcher of Ojibwa culture who "wrote in 1901 that there had been only one case in 25 years' " (101). The age group recalling suicide as a major issue in the community, when "there was always somebody taking themselves out," falls between 40 to 60 years of age. Available records (described above) combined with interview responses from adults and elders point to the mid-1950s and 1960s as a probable period for a rise in suicidal ideation and suicide completion. Studies of American Indian suicide conducted in the 1960s and 1970s corroborate this timeline, while associating suicidal behavior with hopelessness, identity conflict, the boarding school era, alcoholism, fractured family structure, and poverty (U.S. Public Health Service, 1969; May and Dizmang, 1974; Shore, 1975).

SA: *What is death?*

SAULT AREA SCHOOLS ADMINISTRATOR: *What is death. . . . Death is the loss of life (he chuckles). It is the end of your time on this planet. And what I believe to be something greater, after life on earth.*

SA: *How do people in the Sault Tribe community treat death or react to death? Or how have you observed people in the Sault tribe community treat death or react to death?*

SAULT AREA SCHOOLS ADMINISTRATOR: *The Sault Ste. Marie and the Sault tribe community is a very tight-knit, well-connected generational community. And so when Tribal members, from what I have seen, react to the loss of life, they mourn. But it's a community event. It's celebration of one's time on earth. And there is an outpouring of everyone.*

SA: *Have you personally viewed, say, a funeral service? Or something [a death-related event] that involved a Sault tribe member?*

SAULT AREA SCHOOLS ADMINISTRATOR: *I'm trying to think back . . . Because my answer is, I've never been to the traditional . . . the traditional funeral that lasts several days . . . I have never been there. Have I been to the funeral service of a Sault tribe member? Absolutely . . . My father-in-law is 100 percent native. I've been to his brother's funeral, I've been to other family members' funerals. So, yes, I have been to a funeral, but not the traditional several-day ceremony.*

SA: *Is there anything specific or anything that you can remember about those experiences? Is there . . . if you wanted to describe . . .*

SAULT AREA SCHOOLS ADMINISTRATOR: *They're traditionally Catholic (chuckles).*

SA: *Okay.*

SAULT AREA SCHOOLS ADMINISTRATOR: *Which I think stems from generations of the Catholic religion, especially on Sugar Island. And the ability of some of the priests to speak Native American languages to work with Native American people generations ago. And so they're . . . every one [funeral] I've been to has been pretty traditional Catholic service.*

SA: *Was the person who presided over that funeral Brother John Haskell?*

SAULT AREA SCHOOLS ADMINISTRATOR: *It was, yep.*

SA: *At St. Isaac Jogues?*

SAULT AREA SCHOOLS ADMINISTRATOR: *Yes, absolutely. And an amazing man that . . . that generations speak of. It's very, very cool. Because students in this building will talk about John and then their parents and grandparents. It's a lineage that ties generations together.*

SA: *Um hmm. Going back on the same question, How have you seen individuals—and this could be students, it could be your fellow coworkers, it could be people in the community that you know of whether they be native or not—how do people react to death?*

SAULT AREA SCHOOLS ADMINISTRATOR: *I'm going to go to . . . I guess suicide first . . . Because it's probably the most tragic form of death in [that] it's viewed as being preventable and typically it's someone who is young. Students search for answers. Staff search to comfort students. We work very, very hard as an administrative team to provide anything and everything, and people want to do whatever they can to help a family that's grieving but also the other students in the building who are also grieving. Right down to sending food, meeting with kids, helping out however they can. And sometimes as staff people . . . the teachers don't take the time they need to process and help themselves heal. Which we have noticed. What you notice when there's a death in the community is that everyone has a way of grieving. But people will also . . . I hate to say judge, but judge the way others grieve. So a student who is emotional by nature becomes even more emotional in a state of grief. When that happens a student who is reserved will judge that student and talk about how they didn't know the person who died as well as I did, or that they weren't really friends with them. And so you have to work through with that reserved kid that everyone grieves in their own way, and this is their time to do that. And it's not our job to judge how they perceive death, or the things that they need to work through. It's our job to support them. And staff are the same way. They'll look at some students and say I really don't think that they should be allowed to leave class to go to the library, for example, where there's trained mental health professionals to work through this. And the answer I always have is everybody grieves in a different way. And the same thing occurs with helping your staff grieve or grieving with your staff. When you have some people who want to talk to others, some want to go home. Some don't believe in sharing how they're feeling or want to handle it with other people. Some want to tell everybody exactly what they're feeling. As adults, we've set our course in life and we know more or less our destination that we're heading, especially in this field. But teachers are planners, and they don't plan for tragedy. Because we don't want to think about it. It doesn't fit into your lesson plan book, and you don't want it to ever happen. And therefore, when something tragic happens, they want to help however they can, but they want somebody to really help them help everybody else.*

SA: *If you have any memories or any history that you find disturbing, feel free at any point to pause the interview or to ask me to pause the interview.*

SAULT AREA SCHOOLS ADMINISTRATOR: *Okay.*

SA: *Just to let you know.*

SAULT AREA SCHOOLS ADMINISTRATOR: *Okay.*

SA: *I know that administrators such as yourself are hard skinned and have been through the gamut.*

SAULT AREA SCHOOLS ADMINISTRATOR: *I appreciate that.*

SA: *But I've had to say that more times than I thought I would already, so. What happens when a person dies? And that . . . and of course answer that however you wish to, but there's two things that might help with that. There's the actual person who has passed [what happens to the individual?] And the second way to answer that, if you wanted, is what happens within the community afterwards? So, what happens when a person dies?*

SAULT AREA SCHOOLS ADMINISTRATOR: *I think you go through a cycle of grief, um . . . And it starts with shock. 'I can't believe that happened.' 'What happened?' 'Why did it happen?' Especially if you're looking at youth. And if you are looking at youth . . . you go from shock to . . . as a building there's a . . . after the shock comes a, 'I wish they were here,' 'you didn't know them as well as I knew them.' There are the memories, but in youth especially there seems to be a competition for memories. Who was closer to the person? Who knew what they would do in that instance? There's always at that point too, but at the shock point, a preponderance to remember everything good that a person has done. After tragedy the negatives always seem to go away and the positives always seem to flourish. And as a person we all have our negatives and our positives, but there seems to be a glorification at that point of everything good that has happened with that person. And then for real close friends, there seems to be a . . . a question of why you and why not someone else along the way. For a lot of youth we had pass away—well, none of them were suicide, they're all other tragedies—but there seems to be in the last 15 years a preponderance to start a Memorial scholarship type of situation, and that becomes very difficult too as time passes. And you don't, you remember as a friend or family member this person. And they were so sweet and so nice and were taken tragically, and yet the students who are coming up every year remember them less and less, until they're just a name on a plaque. And um, that's a very, very difficult cycle to work through with staff, parents, awardees of the scholarship. It's . . . memories stop at that point. And so, seven or eight years later your memory is exactly the same as it was the day that person passed away. And that's . . . you can watch the rest of their classmates grow older, go to university, join the military, grab a job in town, grow up, get married, start a family. Your memory stops at 16. And the propensity to compare that to today's 16-year-old student is . . . is very difficult.* [PC1/072415]

SA: *What happens when a person dies?*

GOVERNMENT ADMINISTRATOR: *Death is a part of living. And you're going to see each other again. So . . . You can see each other on the other side.*

SA: *Um hmm. Okay.*

GOVERNMENT ADMINISTRATOR: *. . . and that's okay. You walk on to the spirit world and I'll see you there later. That's how I believe.*

SA: *So what happens when a person dies, to the person?*

GOVERNMENT ADMINISTRATOR: *To the per— What happens to the person?*

SA: *Um hmm*

GOVERNMENT ADMINISTRATOR: *Well, their spirit leaves their body but the spirit is . . . their spirit hangs around. Don't you get visits? I do.* [PC2I1/072415]

SA: *Let's say that there was a youth suicide or a suicide whether someone was young or not. how would or how has a traditional healer been involved in that, that process once that event has taken place?*

CULTURAL PROGRAMS ADMINISTRATOR/HELPER: *Once that happens [death] those families will usually call . . . those . . . those traditional families anyway, will call and ask for help. Because they have to . . . they have to do that changing world ceremony for that person. They have to figure out how they're going to do that . . . and still remain sensitive to the issue. So they would call their . . . their pipe person, their teacher, their prayer man or prayer person . . . and he'll go over and talk to that family, and they'll talk with that family, and they'll talk about the . . . the suicide itself. They'll talk about the possibilities of what can be done during that ceremony. But then, they're there. They continue to watch those families. And even more so after the funeral ceremony is done. That aange-kii, that changing world ceremony. And once that's done, whoever those pipe people are, they still have to go back to that family. For months, sometimes years after and be available for . . . for counsel. Or just to be an ear. Because sometimes people, all they need to do is just to get it out, they don't need a response. They don't need some big mystical answer as to why it happened. Sometimes they just need someone to . . . to let it out with. And our traditional people, that's a good thing for our traditional people, because we have that way of trying to take some of that sadness and then we have to go away from there and take care of all of that. We have to use our medicines, we have to use our prayers, you know, to kind of turn that around. But there's, for the cultural community and the spiritual community, it's more about surrounding that family at that time. When we have, when we have a funeral there's a fire that burns for four days, or from the time that they pass until the time they go in the ground that fire will be lit. And it's the tribe will pay for all the wood, the tribe has provided a place to do that. But the community has to step up and it's their time now to take care of these families. These young boys that have been here for 9 out of 10 days, you know, did that. They offered their time. They could've been out fishing or playing video games or basketball, and all of these other things that are available . . . they stayed here. Not only because of the fire, not only because they, you know, they get cigarettes or whatever, but they're mostly here to keep an eye on their family. Whatever family is here. Whether they have problems with that family or not, they still have that dedication. When it's time for ceremony, it's time for ceremony. None of that other stuff matters. And . . . so like I say when this happens, whether it's suicide, whether it's old age or it's a car accident, however that is when they pass, as a community our responsibility as a traditional community is to surround those families. Which means those fire keepers, they're going to take care of that end. There's going to be people that aren't related that are going to be bringing in food. And that's their responsibility. There are people that do prayer, they'll do that, and they'll share some teachings with those families. But they don't even have to listen to that, you know. Again, that goes back to free choice. But that's a part of what we offer is that time, that counsel and that prayer. And also most times, there is no compensation for that. That's just me taking care of my community. Being a part of this community, I feel like I have a responsibility so . . . I was taught about the changing world ceremony. I was taught about fire, I was taught about smudging, I was taught about our medicines. And what we learn these things it's our responsibility to teach them. So like for yourself, you have a basic knowledge of the four colors and the medicines to go with them and how we use that, okay. Well, now it is your responsibility to teach that when you can. If somebody asks, well, why is this yellow, you should be able to have an answer for that, you know. And then that becomes a teachable moment where you can share that whole thing with them. You know, if the time . . . is allowed.* [PC10/080415]

What Is Death?

Before embarking on field research in the Sault Tribe community, my advisors challenged the entirety of my research framework with one simple, yet powerful question: To the Ojibwa, what is death? The longest subsection of interview questions and the crux of this research leaned heavily on that single question. The community filled the initial void of information created by the question "what is death?" by sharing and displaying the Ojibwa cosmology or cultural worldview of death.

Responses to questions of "what is death?" and "how do individuals/the community (Tribal and non-Tribal) respond to death?" yield insight on attitudes toward death, remembrance or memorialization of the dead and further classifications of death. Death, generally speaking, is understood by the Tribal and non-Tribal community as not a definitive ending of one life. Rather, the Ojibwa concept of death is understood as a "changing of worlds" or a transition from a physical world and a biological body to a spiritual world that leaves the 'biological self' behind, allowing a continuation of a spiritual life. Many Tribal and non-Tribal families, as mentioned earlier, ascribe to Christian beliefs and conduct funerals according to a Christian format. For example, a Catholic funeral would consist of a wake or viewing of the body, a church service complete with a eulogy and a mass, and the burial, which, according to Catholic belief, must take place within three days of death. Changing of worlds ceremony, however, includes more steps and community involvement in the funerary process.

When released from the physical body, the spirit is received by ancestors who guide the person to the spiritual world. As the ancestors guide the spirit, it is very common for Tribal members to light a sacred fire to help guide or 'light' the way for the spirit, as the spirit travels toward the ancestors and on to the spirit world. In the time it takes to arrive at the spirit world, however, those who have 'walked on' may visit relatives and friends. Therefore the time immediately after physical death is considered not only an emotionally sensitive period, but a spiritually sensitive period prone to visitations that assist in making peace with losing a loved one. To assist in traditional funerals, Pipe Carriers, also called "helpers" to the people, are included within the funeral process to ensure the emotional stability of family and friends, while leading the ceremonial aspects of the funeral, such as keeping the sacred fire lit, presenting prayers and songs, and teaching friends, family, and other helpers about important ceremonies.

Outside of funerary contexts, however, reactions to suicide display further classifications of death: (1) general death, or a death that is explainable and may be expected, and (2) tragic or untimely death, or a death that is unexplainable, may cause or perpetuate psychological harm for family and friends, and may include a sudden death or an unexpected death. Examples of general death include dying of old age, natural death (cancer), or death resulting from an accident where culpability is not a factor. In effect, the road was slippery and 'accidents happen.'

Interviewees indicate that whether by sudden death from an accident or natural cause (physical ailment, cancer), deaths involving youth are tragic; mainly because regardless of cause, a person has died before his or her time. Suicide, however, separates itself from accidental or natural causes of death in that a sense of mystery often circles the event, while family members, friends, and community members may "shoulder some blame" for the loss of life (see Walls, Hautala, and Hurley, 2014: 65).

The Tribal and non-Tribal community, particularly within the school system, memorializes tragic death in multiple ways—memorial scholarships, physical memorials, more immediate and temporary forms of memorial in places associated with the deceased, such as a school locker. A Sault Area Schools counselor describes the process of remembrance, which commonly centers on discussion of the deceased, revisiting personal connections with the decease, espousing imagined connections, memories of personal interaction and camaraderie, creation of physical memorials, and visiting memorial sites:

SA: How would a person be remembered or thought of after a completed suicide?

COUNSELOR: Well working with the [XXXX] that I'm on, we try to not memorialize, so to speak. Like, even here at the school, we didn't want the locker decorated, we didn't want the, you know, a memorial of any kind done. I mean a youth that dies in an accident, that's happened in the past. You know, the locker's been decorated, there's been a bulletin board. But you don't want to glamorize it. You want to remember and be respectful but you don't want to focus on the how. Just that the life is lost. And be supportive to the family that are left behind.

SA: So the difference, and correct me if I'm wrong, the difference between someone who dies, whether it's a youth or not, who has what would be considered an untimely death, a car accident, something along those lines, and someone who completes suicide . . . one difference that could be seen there is that the community has a movement towards memorializing, memoir, words . . . making a memorial out of it, right?

COUNSELOR: Yes.

SA: So it's more acceptable to make a memorial for somebody who has died in a car accident than someone who's completed a suicide?

COUNSELOR: You see it a lot. I personally don't like it. I . . . remember, yes. [I agree with] Respect [for the deceased], yes. But I don't like the crosses on the side of the road where somebody died, that's not where that person is. The lockers are not where that person is. You keep them in your heart and you have a place to go and remember them when they're buried. So I personally am not a fan of those things. But that's just my thing. But you see it throughout the community everywhere

SA: How do young people respond to the memorials? Do they support it, do they not support it? Do they interact with memorials, I mean the actual . . . let's say there's a locker that has a picture or something like that. Do they, how do they interact with those memorials after a person has died?

COUNSELOR: I think in the beginning, they support that and they go there for comfort, I would say. Because a lot of them go there and leave notes. I think it helps them with the grieving process. But then there are some who shy away from that. Especially youth that are related to that person, you know, if there's a family member within the school. I know that that's extremely hard as a constant reminder that that person's not there anymore. So it's kind of a Catch-22. It helps some kids.

SA: Um hmm.

COUNSELOR: And then some kids it doesn't because it's that reminder that that person's gone now.

SA: You said that those who are most closely related to the person who has, who died. That they shy away from those memorials or those activities.

COUNSELOR: Um hmm.

SA: Why is it that the people who are most closely related seem to shy away in your experience, yet those who, would you describe those who attach themselves, right, or have an attachment to a memorial or to, to something like that . . . how would you describe those people first off, anyways?

COUNSELOR: The ones that attach, I think those are the ones who are a little more attention seeking, a little more needy. They may have some issues going on and they feel that they can identify with this. And those kids are the kids that, you know, we will go pay attention to because they are expressing something then, so they're opening a door. It's giving you an opportunity to go and make contact with that kid even if it's just sitting there talking to them about the memorial. Then they may open up personally and let you know if there's something going on with them. If they're overly distraught, if you know, they're just standing there looking at it, whatever the case may be. It gives you that window of opportunity for those kids that seem to be more at risk for the same kind of behaviors. And a lot of them are, you know, those ones that are needy, the attention seekers. And then you have some that are just that, they just want the attention, there's nothing going on with them other than they want the attention. And

> you know we've had that, where they're not students that are at risk for any kind of at-risk behavior, you know, suicide, drinking, or anything like that, they're just kids that like to be the center of attention. And that's those kids and then . . . so it's distinguishing what kid you have there and you work around here long enough you get to know who's who. [PC52/081215]

While immediate family members and close friends, according to the school counselor, may "shy away" from memorials, many youth who may not have a close or regular personal connection to the deceased may espouse such an attachment. Such displays may be the result of multiple scenarios, alone or in combination. Youth may see a tragic event as an opportunity to seek and gain attention and relief regarding previous and ongoing emotional stress. Youth may also see memorialization as attention seeking behavior or a form of competition for a place in the memorialization process, and thus, social status and social inclusion in the social process of remembering. In a similar vein, youth who are denied options for personal success may see suicide and tragic death as a viable route to being remembered. Suicide can become a "criteria for social inclusion in groups of youth," as well as a "sanctioned reference point for the emerging self, a way to become a memorable person" (Niezen, 2015).

Note

1 Michigan Department of Health and Human Services Vital Records and Health Statistics Section. U.S. Census Bureau, Quick Facts Chippewa County, Michigan. 2010, 2015. Accessed January 31, 2017 www.census.gov/quickfacts/table/RHI325215/26033,26

Works Cited

Almendrala, A. (2015) "Native American Suicide Rates are at Crisis Levels." Huffington Post. Healthy Living.

Basso, K. (1996) *Wisdom sits in Places: Landscape and Language Among the Western Apache*. Albuquerque: University of New Mexico Press.

Brown, D. (1970) *Bury My Heart at Wounded Knee: An Indian History of the American West*. New York: Picador.

Dizmang, L. H., Watson, J. W., and May, P. A. (1970) "Youth Suicide at Fort Hall Indian Reservation." Paper presented at the Annual Meeting of the American Psychiatric Association, San Francisco, CA, May 1970. Typescript. 13 pp., 2 tables.

Dunphy, C. "Young Natives Hopeless Existence; Parents in Isolated Northern Ojibwa Community Reeling Under the Impact of Rash of Suicides." The Ottawa Citizen. March 23, 1993.

Guerra, J. "The devastating rate of suicide among American Indian teens." State of Opportunity: Can Kids in Michigan Get Ahead? Michiganradio.org. November 26, 2014.

Herne, M., Bartholomew, M., and Weahkee, R. (2014). Suicide Mortality Among American Indians and Alaska Natives, 1999–2009. *American Journal of Public Health*, 104(3), S336–342.

Hilger, M. I. (1951) *Chippewa Child Life and Its Cultural Background*. Washington, DC: U.S. Government Print Offices.

Horwitz, S. (2014) "The Hard Lives–And High Suicide Rate–of Native American Children on Reservations." *The Washington Post*.

MacNeil, M. (2008) "An Epidemiologic Study of Aboriginal Adolescent Risk in Canada: The Meaning of Suicide." *Journal of Child and Adolescent Psychiatric Nursing*. 21 (2), 3–12.

May, P., and Dizmang, L. (1974) "Suicide and the American Indian." *Psychiatric Annals*. 4 (11), 22–23, 27–28.

Michigan Department of Community Health (2011) "(Suicide in Michigan: A Hidden Health Issue Suicide Rates by Age and Sex Michigan, 2007–2009." Accessed February 1, 2017. www.michigan.gov/documents/mdch/suicide_fact_sheet_region_8_final_390537_7.pdf

Niezen, Ronald. (2015). "The Durkheim-Tarde Debate and the Social Study of Aboriginal Youth Suicide." *Transcultural Psychiatry* 52 (1) 96–114.

Public Health Service (1969) *Suicide Among the American Indians: Two Work-Shops*. Washington, DC: U.S. Government Printing Office. Publication no. 1903, 36 pp.

Resnik, H. L. P., and Dizmang, L. H. (1970) "Observations on Suicidal Behavior Among American Indians." Paper presented at the Annual Meeting of the American Psychiatric Association, San Francisco, CA, May 1970. Mimeograph. 13 pp. (1971) *Transcultural Psychiatry*. 8 (1), 87–89.

Sault Tribe, Grant Application. "Sault Tribe Alive Youth (STAY) Project 2008." Grant #1U79SM058400-01. OIA. Accessed August 10, 2014.

Shore, J. (1975) "Abstracts and Reviews: American Indian Suicide: Fact and Fantasy." *Psychiatry*. 38 (1), 86–91.

Straight, B., Pike, I., Hilton, C., & Oesterle, M. (2015). Suicide in Three East African Pastoralist Communities and the Role of Researcher Outsiders for Positive Transformation: A Case Study. *Culture, Medicine, and Psychiatry, 39* (3), 557–578.

Trafzer, C. E., Keller, J. A. and Sisquoc, L. (2006) *Boarding School Blues: Revisiting American Indian Educational Experiences*. Edited and with an Introduction by C. E. Trafzer, J. A. Keller and L. Sisquoc. Indigenous Education. Lincoln; University of Nebraska Press.

Walls, M., Hautala, D., Hurley, J. (2014) "Rebuilding our community": Hearing Silenced Voices on Aboriginal Youth Suicide." Transcultural Psychiatry. 51 (1) 47–72.

Vital Records and Health Statistics Section, State of Michigan, Department of Health and Human Services. (Requested, Received August, 2015) "Suicide Deaths by Sex and Age, Chippewa County Residents, 1970–2013" for "All Races," and "American-Indian/Alaska Native."

. . . We work quickly to untie, lift, and carry the twenty-foot flat bottom aluminum boat from the back of the truck to the riverbank. We then place the spear, lantern, C-clamp, and lantern mount, and the kill stick (a short, heavy stick so aptly named because of its purpose, which is to thwack a fish near its eardrum, concussing it to death in order to stop its noisy SOS to other fish) in the boat.

The last slice of sunlight sinks below the horizon, plunging the world into a starry darkness. We march up the porch steps to pay a visit to our uncle. Before knocking on the storm door, the inner door opens and the spry, white-haired man says, "Whattaya want?"

He can contain his comical sense of seriousness for a second before he breaks into a smile and holds the storm door wider, beckoning us, "Come on in and have a seat."

We follow our orders and shuffle inside, gratefully accepting cups of fresh coffee and wooden chairs around the kitchen table. As usual, his home is nearly immaculate. The linoleum kitchen floor is swept clean, the carpeted area still shows the tell-tale tracks of a vacuum cleaner (yes, us Indians can even track appliances through the wilds of our living rooms). Picture frames filled with children, grandchildren, and our recently departed and much admired Aunt are hung about or placed around the house. Books, magazines, and various knick-knacks are also strewn in an organized fashion. The sink is clear of dirty dishes.

After decades of retirement from long-haul trucking, mainly out of industrial southern Michigan, Uncle Mike always struck me as the most industrious of my four uncles. Even in his mid-seventies, the idea of "retirement" seems to elude him. He can often be caught clearing brush on his property and setting fish nets in the river in the summer, or plowing snow in the cold months at a pace that would exhaust most twenty-somethings.

"You wanna come out with us, Uncle?," asks CJ.

"No, I . . . " He almost hesitates. "No, I can't do 'er tonight. My knee is still healing," he says, referring to a recent knee surgery.

"Yeah, you don't want to mess that up. Gotta let stuff like that rest if you want it to heal right," I says.

"Yeah, the doctor said I really had to take it easy with it. I wish I could go out with you boys, though. Last year's was a heck of a night. You remember that?," he says, pointing to me.

"Yeah that was pretty cool."

"I never saw a sturgeon that close."

"You guys saw a sturgeon out here?" asks CJ.

"Yeah," says Uncle Mike, "Came right under our boat and circled us three or four times. Man, I'm glad you didn't spear that one."

"I almost did," I say. "I looked out and thought, 'Is that a boulder moving? Am I seeing things?' But when I realized it was moving, I didn't know what to think. I turned to Uncle Mike and said, 'There's something big out there moving toward us.'"

"And I told him, 'Well, what is it?'"

"'I don't know,' I says, 'but whatever it is, it's bigger than any fish I've ever seen.' And he says, 'well, spear it!'"

"Did you try to spear it?" asks CJ.

"No way," I says. "As it came closer and we saw the spots on its back and the skin instead of scales, we knew it was a sturgeon."

"If you woulda speared that, we'd've been dragged to the East Coast before it stopped. That thing was . . . how big would you say it was?"

"Jeez, probably around five feet long and nearly three feet wide. And that isn't even as big as they get," I says.

"That woulda been a lot of meat though. And probably a pretty high price per pound, considering how the fine for spearing a sturgeon without a permit," says CJ with a chuckle.

"The only way I know of to spear a sturgeon is to use two boats and two spears, and even then the spears that we had would've shivered," says Uncle Mike. "Or you can turn the spear so the tines go long-ways so they sink right in the middle of its head along the spot where the bony plates come together. That's the only weak spot it has where you can land a shot in the brain and kill it immediately."

"But that would've been a lucky strike," I says. "I just thought it was pretty neat, seeing that big sturgeon circle the boat and the lantern light within arm's reach."

"Yeah, that was pretty neat," says Uncle Mike. A short silence falls among us after the description of the encounter with the prehistoric giant, a greatly reduced number of which still lurk in the river. "Well, you guys better get out there if you want to get a full night's in."

With a good luck from our Uncle, we pick our way across the yard to the boat. After putting the gear, ores, and the 10-foot spear along the inside of the wall, we take positions on the sides and lift it partially into the water. I step in and make my way to the back over two rows of seating. CJ and Matt push the boat out further and CJ files in. CJ and I push with ore and spear-butt, while Matt, in his knee-high boots, finishes pushing us out until we are free of land and barely floating above the sandy, pebbly river bottom. He steps in and, weighted with over six hundred pounds of men, the small aluminum craft gently begins to drift out into the small bay.

CJ lights the gas lantern and hands it to me, instructing me how to hang it onto the post clamped to the aft wall. With the lantern hanging precariously over the water, we paddle out into deeper water.

Spearing is a fun thing to do, but probably a funnier thing to see. Originally, Ojibwa men would paddle out in birch bark canoes and spear fish by the light of torches held in place at the end of the canoe. I am not sure where the idea came from, but I would have loved to be in on that conversation. In my mind it goes something like this:

'Hey, you know how fire and boats don't mix?'

'Yeah.'

'And how standing in a canoe can lead to impromptu swimming lessons?'

'Uh-huh.'

'Well, I have an idea . . . Let's put a small fire on one end of a canoe, paddle it out to the middle of a river, stand up, and try to spear fish as they pass by.'

'Yeah, I like fish. Let's do that.'

A part of me has to believe I am related to one of the people involved in this conversation.

In place of a torch, we now use a gas lantern, or even regular household light bulbs placed precariously in the river and held in place above the water by a floating board, which is powered by a car-battery (electricity being another thing that does not mix well with aquatic activities). Supposedly, the fish are attracted by the light and are that much easier to spear; though I have yet to see a fish purposefully come to the light or be stunned by the light in some close-encounter-of-the-fourth-kind scenario.

The person who is spearing stands completely upright on the back of the boat, searching the twenty-foot arch of illumination.

The pilot sits on the opposite end and paddles according to the direction of the spearman. So the boat is literally being paddled backwards. Directing the boat towards unsuspecting fish or intercepting a moving target requires a lot of communication between the spearman and the pilot. If you were a third person in the boat, as I was now, you could keep an eye out and in the event a fish is speared and carefully lifted into the boat, beat its head with the aforementioned "kill stick," in order to keep it from warning its buddies of their impending doom.

CJ is the first one up to spear and Matt the pilot. So I wait my turn to spear or pilot and chew on jerky in the center of the boat.

CJ tells Matt to "take her straight out for a while." As we make our way at a crawling pace, CJ gives directions to avoid the large rocks and boulders strewn along the river floor, some of which poke out of the water, and others barely remain submerged for the unsuspecting. Thousands of years ago the receding glaciers left great boulders in their wake; though from another view it looks as if God decided to play a game of marbles eons ago and forgot to pick them up. After about twenty minutes, we come to the spot CJ guided us to. Two small islands, perhaps a hundred feet long and fifty wide and covered with brush and stunted pines, have made good spots for spearing in the past. They also made for fun adventuring, and as kids we kicked out on driftwood to explore them.

We keep our eyes peeled on the water, searching for the slightest shift in the shadows or flicker of a tail that would indicate a pike, walleye, trout, bass, or perch. The silence is only broken by minuscule drips of water from the ore, which Matt expertly wields. CJ holds the spear as a high-wire artist would for balance.

For nearly an hour, we circle the islands and make our way eastward along the shallows, never drifting past depths of four or five feet. The wind, thankfully, keeps calm. Wind-borne ripples can make spearing all but useless, but are held at bay tonight. Perhaps there was something to offering the tobacco in the water before setting off.

Eventually, CJ and I switch and I take my turn standing with the spear poised over the water. For all of my concentration, I cannot see a thing that resembles a fish other than the notorious "stickfish"—small logs and branches that can look deceivingly like a fish, especially when one wants so badly to see something.

In the cool silence of the night we drift like lonely ghosts, lit by the eerie glow of the lantern. Lonely, because during the many times that I have speared on the river, I have not once seen another boat chasing aquatic game along the shoreline. Every house, every person, and everything is asleep but us, the fish who dance playfully in and out of our light, and the river with its many sounds. Deliberately, strategically, meticulously we weave around islands, follow stream heads to their terminus, and even search under private docks and boats in our inspection. Fish tend to move along the edges of underwater plants and rocks, as opposed to being out in the open of the sandy bottom areas; and so then do we.

Over two ours have passed. We have cycled between pilot, middle person, and spearman at least twice each. CJ had a stab at a quickly moving perch, and we had a few sightings on the murky edges of the light, but all in all the only significant event occurred when I almost tipped into the water while trying to take a piss.

Losing faith in the eastern stretch of the river, we turn about and begin on the long trek westward, aiming for the landing at Uncle Mike's. Matt takes the spear, CJ the paddle in the back, and I the lazy seat in the middle. Caught up in the simple bliss of yet more beef jerky and the brilliant stars set above us and reflecting against the calm water, I didn't notice it. And even if I had seen it out of the corner of my eye, I would've dismissed it as just another small log that resembled a fish. But Matt and CJ were quick to realize that it was not a log, even though they too had to do a double-take . . .

Drawn Away

So many attempted suicides
They filled up the [hospital] wards
It's very economically depressed
There's nothing much for the kids
We've lost a lot of our spirituality
And our guidance in our lives
Kids don't really have anything to fall back on.

I try to encourage them to get on the drum,
Attend sweat lodges.
They were caught up in the same problems that the rest of society has.
Even though they're exposed to the positives,
The spirituality,
They are also exposed to negatives.
They've been drawn away.

[The children are] exposed
To substance abuse
And unstable, dysfunctional family
Even though they were exposed to the traditions
That has an effect
Throughout their lives
It's really hard for 'em to break that.

They have to leave to find decent jobs and work
You find that going back two generations
And they lose their culture.
Mother, she would bring up things from my youth on Sugar Island,
My ancestral home.
People would gather there.
You would get culture from that.

Anishnaabemowin . . .
[the Ojibwa] language
She wouldn't, she didn't want to teach me.
Children my age
Their parents didn't want to teach the language.
Being known as Indian
Would hold you back in life.

People would try to hide
That they were native
By calling themselves French-Canadian
Or Spanish
Not Indian
Really you're only fooling yourself.
Everybody knew who you were anyways.

I asked my mother what French-Canadian was
And she was kind of . . . embarrassed we did that.
"*Oh, you know, that's a . . . a way that people can try to hide*
That they are Indian"
And I says, "*why do they do that?*
They're Indian aren't they?"
I didn't understand.

Poem formed from conversation with Sault Tribe member, born 1950s [PC00/011314]

My father was very light. He had white skin and white hair from a very early age. He used to try to darken it [his skin] by not wearing shirts and hats and by jumping into cold water, while my mother was dark skinned and used to try to lighten her skin by always wearing hats and bonnets and long sleeves.

Keewaydinoquay: Stories from My Youth (2006: 31)

An old woman and what looks to be her granddaughter timidly enter the lodge and stand just inside the low entrance to the domed structure. I watch them from my seat near the Eastern Door, as they peer hesitantly into the dim interior, which is lit by the orange flames of a small fire within and bright daylight cast through the door from without. I recognize the little eight- or nine-year-old girl by her red regalia as the talented shawl dancer that I saw earlier that day.

A tall, somewhat rotund male elder squeezes past them and walks toward the sacred fire at the center of the lodge. Four stumps, each two feet high, are placed around the fire at the four directions. Atop the platforms are bowls containing the four Sacred Medicines. He takes a pinch of Semaa (Tobacco) from the Easternmost bowl, closest to the physical opening, and feeds the offering into the flames in a swirling motion. He travels around the fire clockwise, stopping at the Southern, Western, and Northern points, gently collecting the medicines from each bowl and scattering the sacred plants into the fire in the same quiet manner. Completing his circular journey, he exits.

After he leaves, the old woman gestures towards the fire and medicines and asks, "Can you show us how to do this?" Knowing they had observed the elder, I motioned towards the departing man and advised them to "do what he was doing."

They were still timid. I explained, briefly and according to my limited knowledge, what it means to put down or place in the sacred fire Semaa, Spruce, Sweetgrass, and Sage, and which door each medicine is associated with—the Eastern, Southern, Western, and Northern doors, respectively. And what it is to travel around the lodge in a clockwise manner, as a representation of time. And that People do things differently, but that the offering of Semaa, Sage, Sweetgrass, and Spruce are given in prayer, which is then carried up with the smoke.

Looking at the grandmother and the granddaughter and their very strong Native features, I was reminded of something that the elderly man who just departed said to me the evening before. Sitting together under the tin roof pavilion which was recently built for the pow-wow grounds, I asked, "Why do you think people come here? Do you think that people who come to these events . . .

do you think they come here for some personal meaning, to find something?"

"Yeah, I can believe that. People come here because a lot of them . . . some of them do traditional things all the time, but some are not traditional. Are from downstate or other places, and they want to keep this within their identity."

Later that afternoon it gets near time to leave, and I begin searching for my nephew . . . [FN10/071815]

3 What Is an "Indian"? Conflicted Identity in the Sault Tribe

> *People, if they have a purpose they don't do those kinds of things [suicide], okay? They have a reason to get up in the morning . . . That'll cause all kinds of prevention, just by having a direction and a purpose and a responsibility. A fire keeper, his job is to learn about those medicines, to learn about the fire, to learn about all of the etiquette that goes along with that in taking care of the fire. You fill your time and you fill your life with sacrifice. You fill your life with that dedication to teaching whoever it is that asked. That's a good way. And then we won't have that suicide anymore. That's my hope.*
>
> — Sault Tribe Member, Prayer Person and Resident of Eastern Upper Peninsula Area [PC10/080415]

A common belief amongst many Bowheting Ojibwa is that youth suicide intrinsically relates to sense of purpose and identity for individual Tribal members and community as a whole. The role of identity, and the impact that historical trauma, symbolic violence, racism, and structural violence can have on multiple levels of (self) perception of indigenous peoples and the construction of indigenous identity is fast becoming a major feature in studies of suicide, self-harm, and prevention (Neizen, 2015; Walls, Hautala, and Hurley, 2014). During collaborative research on the relationship between self-harm and substance abuse amongst the White Mountain Apache, Barlow et al. (2012) altered the research design to recognize the "local understanding that suicidal and substance abuse behaviors are alien to Apache traditions" and that self-harm and substance abuse

> may share common root causes residing in a multigenerational history of trauma that eroded protective factors embedded in Apache culture. Tribal stakeholders seek understanding as to whether both behaviors may function as self-annihilation that arises in adolescence when vulnerable youth struggle to *consolidate identity* during the transition to adulthood.
>
> (404, italics added)

The need to explore identity-loss as a potential risk factor is supported by studies displaying the opposite effect—that is, personal and ethnic identity can become a strong protective factor for community and individual health and wellbeing (Broad, Boyer, and Chattaway, 2006; Angell, Kurz, and Gottfried, 1998). Researchers and indigenous communities are also pushing for more exploration of identity within behavioral health evaluation and treatment approaches (Goodkind et al., 2010). Despite the recent attention paid to one's relationship with identity, identity in and of itself is rarely understood independently of youth suicide, prior to attaching any significance of Tribal identity to suicide. While many historical works are available for social scientists and indigenous communities to reference, such as Berkhofer's classic *White Man's Indian* (1978), such works cannot replace a social and historical mapping of the twists and turns of identity construction in specific communities. Informed by the viewpoints of the community and recent developments in the literature, this study attempts to fill the gap in indigenous suicide research with interview questions and field observations that revolve around identity. What seem like basic questions, however—"What is an Indian?", "What does it mean to be Ojibwa?", and "How do Tribal members display or act out their identity?"—result in answers that are anything but.

Everyday nuances of self and ethnic identity, most effectively illustrated through qualitative research (i.e., ethnography), are often pushed aside in favor of quantitative methods of data collection and analysis. As a result, we have a poor understanding of the potential role of identity within indigenous health. The subject of identity, and any explicit or implicit impact that identity has on suicide in the Sault Tribe, deserves more time and energy than what is available in this short study. However, reviewing responses to interview questions, ethnic observations, and historical documents relating to the Bowheting Ojibwa yields a portrait of Ojibwa identity that is complex and conflicted, as well as resilient and healing.

How the Bowheting Ojibwa—or the Sault Tribe, Anishnaabek, Indians, Native Americans, American Indian/Alaska Natives residing in and around Sault Sainte Marie, Michigan—display or act out the 'Tribal Self' and Tribal history is incumbent on the physical and social contexts. That is, Tribal identity relies on the circumstance(s) at the time, be they political, ceremonial, patriotic-nationalistic, contemporary Pan-Indian or inter-tribal, or historical contexts. Visible examples of the effect of different contexts on Tribal identification can be found in the name of the community itself, while more implicit relationships with Tribal identity are observed in the everyday expressions of identity and attachments to Tribal history.

The Sault Sainte Marie Tribe of Chippewa Indians—shortened to Sault Tribe of Chippewa Indians or Sault Tribe (pronounced Soo and not to be confused with the Plains Sioux)—is the official title of the community at the center of this study. Sault Tribe is most commonly used during governmental and business-related circumstances. "Sault Tribe Sainte Marie Tribe of Chippewa Indians," however, was preceded by "The Original Bands of Chippewa Indians and Their Heirs," a mid-twentieth-century title for the Ojibwa residents of Sugar Island and the Sault Sainte Marie area, who at the time were pursuing federal recognition. The title changed to its present state upon federal recognition in 1978 (*Story of Our People: The Sault Ste. Marie Tribe of Chippewa Indians*, saulttribe.com, accessed January 9, 2017). The use of Sault Tribe bled into everyday conversation, with Ojibwa people describing themselves as members of the Sault Tribe; a title that stands opposite to what many consider the 'traditional' alternatives, *Ojibwa* or *Anishnaabek*.

In oral histories and within Anishnaabemowin (also Ojibwamowin), the language of the Ojibwa, Tribal members are described as *Ojibwa*, a separate Tribal entity. Ojibwa people also call themselves *Anishinaabek*, which refers to their membership in a larger, multi-Tribal ethnic group comprising the Ojibwa and their Bodwadomii and Odawa cousins (English pronunciation Pottawatomie and Ottawa). Historically known as the "Three Fires," the Anishnaabek share similar oral history and traditions, spiritual practices, family-clan structures, and political systems.

In certain circumstances where Ojibwa people are joined by people of varying indigenous or non-indigenous ethnic backgrounds (physically or in the case of prayer and ceremony, metaphysically), *Anishnaabek* is used to encompass all humans as a species. In effect, Anishnaabek becomes "All People" or "All Humans." Going further, the Ojibwa include animals, plants, natural phenomena, and elements as "brothers," "sisters," "grandfathers," and similar familial terms. Such broad treatment of people, animals, plants, and non-living objects as equally animate illustrates the animistic spiritual beliefs of the Ojibwa and the holistic connection that Ojibwa, as well as non-Western peoples in general, often feel with social, natural, and supernatural environments.

Bowheting, which translates to "Gathering Place at the Falls," is often added to *Ojibwa* or *Anishnaabek* to signify the place-name bestowed on the banks of the Saint Marys River within oral history. Individual Ojibwa or Anishnaabek bands are often identified with special landmarks, ecological systems, and places of significance within oral history. The Anishnaabek of the Upper Great Lakes region, for example, are broadly called *Kitchigamig Anishnaabek* or "People of the Great Lakes" (Teeple and Kamuda, 1994), which emphasizes the proximity of the Anishnaabek to the Great Lakes and the ecological relationship between the various bands of Anishnaabek and the Great Lakes system. The more specific place-name for the *Bowheting Ojibwa* or *Bowheting Anishnaabek*, however, originates from oral history.

According to the migration story, the *Anishnaabek* formerly lived near the Northern Atlantic coast. Before the arrival of the Europeans, Seven Spirits visited the Anishnaabek, bestowing multiple prophecies upon them and instructing them to migrate farther to the west. As the Anishnaabek neared the Saint Marys River, Kitchi Manitou (The Great Spirit) sent Crane to call out with his loud voice and gather the traveling Anishnaabek to the banks and falls of the river, where they would enjoy the plentiful fish and game. The settlement of Bowheting fulfilled one of the instructions given by the Seven Spirits, while other bands of Ojibwa continued on the migration westward, eventually forming communities in Minnesota, Wisconsin, Dakota, and southern Canada.

"The Gathering Place" became an essential meeting point in the summer months, when important ceremonies, trade, and social events took place, and families could take advantage of the seasonal fish run. The military, political, and economic importance of *Bowheting* enhanced when French explorers arrived to trade furs, convert Tribal peoples to Christianity, and continue a low-intensity war against British forces east of the Great Lakes region. To this day, Bowheting remains one of the most important historical and cultural landmarks for the Anishnaabek. Within the Three Fires and individual communities, the Anishnaabek also organize around a clan structure. Based on a supernatural being, each clan holds traditional responsibilities toward their communities. For instance, Bear Clan responsibility is to protect and keep peace within the community, while Crane Clan membership denotes a leadership role. The format for personal introduction captures the complexities of Anishnaabek identity. For example:

> *Anii, Mueshka Mikan Bemosed Indizhnikaaz, Mukwa Dodaim, Bowheting Ndoonjibaa.*
> (Greetings, My name is Man Who Walks the Red Road, I am Bear Clan, my home is at Bowheting [Sault Sainte Marie, Michigan or Canada]).

We can argue, after reviewing the oft-confusing matrix of titles of a Sault Tribe member—or Bowheting Ojibwa person—that the political-official and ethnic identities stand in direct contrast to each other. *Tribe* replaces *People*. *Chippewa* (an Anglicization or twisting of the word Ojibwa to fit the English language) replaces *Ojibwa*. *Bowheting* replaces *Sault Sainte Marie, Michigan*. Finally, a Tribal identification card and enrollment number replace the personalized introduction. At this point, it is fair to ask, "What is in a name?" In answer to that question, names and identities are more than written or spoken designations for social groups. Identity is a visible and verbal representation of how we feel about our sense of purpose. Eventually, identification with certain personas and social groups strongly dictates our attitudes, actions, and physical and mental well-being (Dressler and Bindon, 2000).

Amongst Sault Tribe members, the erosion of culture and loss of language is commonly attributed to the harmful Indian Policy enacted by the American government, with the intention of forceful assimilation into American society. Forced assimilation is a process of pressuring a specific ethnic group into learning and practicing the values, behaviors, language, and norms of a foreign culture. Forced assimilation differs from general assimilation in that a person can choose to assimilate to a dominant society in order to reduce anxiety and gain status and economic benefit. Individuals moving to a foreign country for better opportunities, for instance, choose to enter another cultural sphere and learn traditions, language, and social values for their own benefit without pressure from the foreign society.

The Ojibwa maintained significant political and military control of the Upper Great Lakes region until the Cass Expedition of 1820 and a push for mining and settlement of the Upper Peninsula in the late 1800s. Families migrated between the Saint Marys River and shorelines of the Great Lakes in the summer and inland areas in the winter to take advantage of seasonal food sources—fish, moose, deer, and various wild plants—an active practice even up until the mid-twentieth century. Elders speak of trips between inland hunting cabins and other wooded areas and temporary homes on the river and lakes. The passing on of oral histories, regular use of the Ojibwa language, and important ceremonies, such as fasting, accompanied the migratory lifestyle.

With each broken treaty, unscrupulous land deal that diminished access to hunting and fishing grounds, industrial or mining effort, and restriction of Tribal rights, the relative political and economic freedom that resisted large-scale forced assimilation diminished. The mid-1800s and the late 1900s became a tumultuous period for many Sault Tribe families. Add to this era of land loss political challenges and racialized socioeconomic pressures of the boarding school era, which robbed young children and future generations of traditions, language, and customs that are central to Ojibwa identity.

During the mid- to late twentieth century, indigenous communities in the Upper Peninsula saw a continuation of racial discrimination, poverty, restrictions to low wage labor, alcoholism, and preventable disease in Indian communities. Such factors were everyday realities in the Mar-Shunk neighborhood of Sault Sainte Marie:

> In the late 1960s and early '70s, the Shunk Road and Marquette Avenue area of Sault Ste. Marie had no paved roads, no public housing and no businesses. It provided virtually no public or Tribal services. The roads were so bad that school buses wouldn't pick up children.

> Sault Ste. Marie did not provide water or sewer service to the area. Most of the area was either wetlands or swamp.
>
> (Teeple and Kamuda, 1994)

In order to avoid racial discrimination and negotiate an economic and social environment hostile to non-American people, many Ojibwa eventually learned to adopt the American identity and refuse the Ojibwa self. "Americanization," as it came to be known, not only affected indigenous peoples but was also aimed at incoming European immigrants as a way of replacing or altering foreign values and language to more closely resemble American values and language. The idea behind Americanization was, in essence, to include ethnic groups within the "melting pot" of American culture, thereby eroding strong, identifying characteristics of indigenous and migrant European culture (language, clothing styles, marriage practices, religion, and so on).

Methods for hiding "Indianness" were often dependent on how "Indian" a person or family looked. For instance, a person or family with lighter skin tone could identify as white, while a family or an individual with Native American features might have identified as "French-Canadian or Spanish . . . Not Indian" (see the poem, pp. 83–84) One well-respected elder, with a chuckle, recounted to me his experiences as a Mexican youth, even learning to speak Spanish to fill the role. A woman born in the 1980s describes her experiences:

> My mother grew up in the era where . . . Even my grandfather, my grandfather was in boarding schools. He was one of the elders that was taken from his family and had his hair cut, that kind of thing. So there's that stigma of being native, so my mom didn't identify that way and she didn't raise my brother and I with that mindset that we were native. That we had a heritage out there to explore . . . [PC5I1/081215]

Pressed by a lack of well-paying and reliable employment, many Ojibwa families during this period left their home communities and relocated to industrial areas of southern Michigan (Jackson, 2002). It is reasonable to believe that economically motivated relocation hastened the erosion of traditional Ojibwa values, knowledge, and language and the adoption of American values and norms. For those who stayed in the Eastern Upper Peninsula, however, unemployment and a dearth of alternatives to substance abuse and risky behaviors equated to a sense of despair:

> There are so many, so many times I remember being a kid here growing up and there was nothing . . . nothing to do. Everything around here is geared between, you know, let's say kids up to about 10 years

old. Once you get to that 10 to 13 age bracket, then there's nothing to do until you turn 21 and you can start drinking. So a lot of them begin to practice early. And that becomes very difficult . . . It leads to a lot of different problems, you know, legal problems, substance abuse problems, social problems. And that's because our youth aren't engaged. We don't have a whole lot . . . and . . . I'm thinking this way because I just read an article that was written by one of my great nieces, about finding something else to do. Because our young people in this area . . . we've been a great producer of young people and we've exported [young people]. I'm almost 50 years old and in my whole life, this town has never grown. It hasn't dropped but it hasn't grown. We've gained some, some business. But those jobs are just sucked up by the people that stay. You know, as far as our young people, 13 to 21, there's no future. There's no jobs that opened up. Usually around here if somebody gets a decent job they'll keep it, for as long as they can. So we have always exported our kids. Send them off to go into the military. They go down to work in the factories, or whatever that is. Its those ones that try to stay that have a really hard time. Trying to keep their mind active, trying to keep their bodies active and we just don't have that here. And I don't know what the answer is. Is it a waterpark? Is it [indecipherable]? Is it a dance hall? A pinball place, an arcade or a pool hall or something? There's just not a whole lot to do. And everything that there is to do is too damn expensive for them. There's going to the movies when we could. But that's hard for a kid, they gotta plan that stuff for a month, just to be able to go on one date to a movie with a girlfriend. Other than that, there's nothing to do. Those are some of our core problems with this area. And it has even farther-reaching effects, beyond suicide even. The social problems, the legal problems, the substance abuse, all of these things are symptoms. You know, suicide is one of those . . . one of those symptoms of the social problems they have in here. [Phone rings; not answered.] In my opinion. [PC101/072415]

Many Ojibwa also joined the U.S. military, receiving jobs training, leadership training, and veteran's educational benefits. By the late twentieth century, while parents refused to acknowledge or pass on an indigenous identity, as described above, it is possible that many parents simply did not possess any in-depth knowledge of Ojibwa ancestry, customs, or language to pass on to their children and grandchildren. Through intentional and unintentional methods, including boarding schools, racial discrimination, destruction of natural resources and sources of economy (natural fisheries in the Saint Marys River most notably), and economically pressured relocation, the strategy of "Killing the Indian to save the man" was nearly fulfilled.

It can be argued that historical works and museums (e.g., Museum of Ojibwa culture, Saint Ignace, http://museumofojibwaculture.net/index.html, the River of History Museum, Sault Sainte Marie, Michigan, http://riverofhistory.org/) portray the loss of Ojibwa land, resources, culture, and language in terms of an indigenous versus non-indigenous dichotomy. Such as dichotomy may be colored by Christian missionization, opportunistic political and trade alliances, warfare, colonization, disastrous governmental policies, and racial and ethnic discrimination (e.g., Cleland, 2001, 1992). Unable to use warfare and trade alliance as viable options for defending political sovereignty, indigenous peoples responded to forced assimilation by covertly maintaining ethnic identity in the late nineteenth and early twentieth centuries, with the Red Power Movement, pursuit of treaty rights and federal recognition, and development of new economic opportunities. Despite continued resilience and adapted methods of cultural continuity, Ojibwa identity did not escape the forces of assimilation unscathed—a conclusion that most can agree with. As uncontroversial as that conclusion may be, to rely upon such a simple analysis prevents peering into the depths of indigenous identity. Seeking an often broken sense of belonging and purpose, indigenous individuals and families navigate strong, if hidden, currents of ethnic and racial stereotype, structural violence, and symbolic violence. Perversely, specific aspects of stereotyped identity are accepted and perpetuated within the Ojibwa community, while adapted forms of discrimination are applied to fellow Tribal members in an effort to maintain the 'traditional' Indian identity.

Evidenced through spoken and observed sentiments of Tribal members engaged in cultural activities and recalling identity conflict, the official language of educational and mental health institutions, and the promotion of stereotypical imagery as accepted representations of indigenous identity, such forms of Tribal identification threaten to erode, rather than bolster, social cohesion and sense of belonging amongst Tribal members. The political and economic revitalization of the Sault Tribe, ironically, compounded the maelstrom of Ojibwa identity.

Funding for infrastructure and essential services, conversion of Tribal properties into valuable trust land assets, and gaining longed-for treaty rights and privileges accompanied federal recognition in 1972. Following on the heels of federal recognition were legal victories confirming treaty fishing rights (1978) and religious freedoms (1974) on the national level. Following a Pan-Indian economic trend, casinos broke ground in the 1980s, bringing revenues and increasing quality of life for Tribal members. The results of federal recognition and Tribal industry—new roads, quality housing with electricity and water, local health and dental services, higher education opportunities, and public programs—are a source of great pride for a community that still remembers the days of tar paper shacks absent of electricity and running water and of preventable diseases. Perhaps the most visible center of this transformation was the Mar-Shunk neighborhood, the largest populated reservation area for the Sault Tribe. Essentially, the Sault Tribe transformed reservation lands from what was (and still is for many Native American reservation, or "Rez," communities), a third world reality in a first world country.

Federal recognition, however, brought something else—another way to be "Indian." As resources rolled in, people who previously claimed to be anything but Native lined up to receive an official, government-issued heritage in the form of a Tribal identification card. The process of claiming an official Tribal membership is a relatively easy one due to the Sault Tribe's use of the descendancy system of membership. A person is eligible for membership if he or she can trace a family tree back to a person recorded on a census of Tribal members compiled in 1907, known as the Durant Roll. Once the applicant provides documentation displaying a direct link to an ancestor listed on the Durant Roll, he or she is officially enrolled as a Sault Tribe member. (See Bardill, n.d., for general description of methods of determining Tribal membership.)

A Tribal identification card signifies official Tribal status, marking one as a 'card-carrying Indian.' At times, individuals also express Indian heritage without possessing a Tribal ID by claiming a distant Indian relative (i.e., my great-great grandmother was half-Cherokee). Lacking legitimacy in the form of blood connection to the indigenous community, individual lived experience transecting indigenous history and historical trauma, or validation of Indian identity from elders who "lived it"—"it" being earlier generational stages of Indian history—such claimants may be seen as trespassers on Native identity, or fake Indians (Jackson, 2002).

The inclusion of individuals on Tribal rolls who did not express their "Indianness" before federal recognition is still bitter tea for some Sault Tribe members who, prior to federal recognition, did not shed Ojibwa identity or Tribal status to avoid social and economic discrimination. Staying within more closed circles provided these Ojibwa with a sense of solidarity, ethnic pride, and communal-economic resources. An Ojibwa woman in her 60s states:

> [T]hey all hung around together . . . They all lived near each other. That's who they hung out with . . . That's the way it was. . . . So how could the word racism, you know, [exist in their circles if] they didn't go outside their circles? I remember my grandmother and all those people. I remember how they were treated. Like, there was this bar called the [XXXX]. That's where they all went. It was an Indian bar. And that's where they went. They didn't just go out to any bar because you couldn't. So they stayed in their own circles.
>
> [PC2I1/072415]

Families and individuals who stayed within more expressly "Indian" circles usually lived in close proximity to each other on Sugar Island, near Sault Sainte Marie and the surrounding area. Today, individuals who are related to early members of this circle of Ojibwa families are often easily identified by last name, a few examples being Causelys, Payments, Corbieres, Menards, or dozens of other names that could be listed here.

An individual who is associated with or carries a well-known family name may automatically garner a sense of loyalty, openness, and cooperation from the community, especially elderly community members who are reminded of deep bonds with neighboring families. As a display of direct lineage to local history and Ojibwa heritage, the family name becomes a 'pass card' of sorts. The use of last names to identify family history, relation to members of elder cohorts, and possibly kinship is reminiscent of the Ojibwa clan system.

Individuals who expressed "Indianness" during more discriminatory times are most critical of 'official' and 'fake' Indians. Responding to questions of racism, and race as a source of stigma in the Tribal and non-Tribal community, the Ojibwa woman in her 60s quoted above states: "[W]e got a lot of people in our Tribe who were never Indian before and now they are." Recalling a childhood memory of a visiting writer interviewing her parents and grandparents, she continues:

> I remember a guy doing interviews on it [racism]. He asked [her parents' and grandparents' generation], do you feel racism? [They answered] No. And why didn't they? Because they all hung around together. They all lived near each other. That's the way it was.
>
> [B]ut now that we are opened up so much, and what a Tribe is . . . and it gets pretty ridiculous. I mean . . . I'm sorry, but I remember. I know elders that just cry because these people were never Indian before and they couldn't get in to see somebody [at the health center] because these people who were never Indian before [were using health services] and they used to tease them. Now [the Elders] they're in the waiting room and they can't get in. Yeah, I know people that used to call me squaw all the time and they're Tribal members now. And I just look at them and think, 'read my mind.'
>
> [PC2I1/072415]

The sense of animosity existing between Tribal members who expressed Ojibwa identity, even in times of discrimination, and those who may have pursued official Tribal status to gain benefits may be further exacerbated by the nuances of the Tribal enrollment process; specifically, discussion over the effectiveness of the descendancy system in maintaining Ojibwa heritage and ethnic identity.

An alternative method of enrollment into American Indian and First Nations Tribes emphasizes minimum blood quantum. According to blood quantum enrollment, individuals must meet a minimum percentage of Indian ancestry to be included as full members. A common minimum is 25 percent or "quarter blood." While there is no indication that the Sault Tribe will instate a blood quantum requirement, Sault Tribe members bring up the blood quantum system during informal discussions of Ojibwa genetic and ethnic survival, and possible methods for preempting non-Tribal members from gaining membership purely for personal economic gain. The process of measuring blood quantum is difficult to tell, especially considering that for about four hundred years, Ojibwa people intermarried and had offspring with Europeans, Americans, and other indigenous peoples.

Discussion of a blood quantum standard for acceptance or rejection of individuals in Tribal society, however, may represent a racially based attitude of social inclusion, exclusion, or hierarchy. A "quarter-blood," for instance, while officially accepted into the Tribe, may be seen or see him/herself as a marginally enfranchised Tribal member. As a result, members with lower blood quantum may restrict involvement in cultural activities or ceremonial events as a result of racial attitudes—real or perceived. The same racial attitude may affect Tribal members with a "white" physical appearance—'Look how white I am; I am not taking part/I can't take part in a sweat lodge/pow-wow/pipe ceremony; I don't even look Indian.'

Many Tribal members who lived through periods of more noticeable racism, especially elders, are harsh critics of tying social status to higher blood quantum (i.e., "100 percent," "75 percent," or "50 percent"). Often, elders treat the subject of high blood quantum or percentage, and those who claim a higher blood quantum, with humorous and disarming criticism. During a language class at the Sault Tribe elder center, for example, a junior instructor, a middle-aged woman, joked that she was "moving up in the world" after a review of her blood quantum confirmed she was now 50 percent,Indian. The senior instructor, in his 70s, replied, "Yeah, you went from quarter blood to half blood. And now, as soon as the paperwork goes through, your work ethic is going to drop off." [FN58/072815]

Elders, teachers of cultural knowledge, and spiritual leaders also tend to ignore physical appearance or previous involvement in cultural practices as the basis for teaching traditional knowledge and acknowledgement of individuals as Tribal members. The only prerequisites for requesting particular knowledge or teaching is a humble demeanor and an offering of tobacco. Teachers and spiritual leaders also accept non-Tribal people curious about 'Indian culture'; depending, of course, on their level of sincerity and respect for Tribal norms. While an attitude of tolerance and acceptance could be called an Ojibwa cultural trait, elders also view "putting culture out there" as strategically important. At the Sugar Island Pow-Wow and Spiritual Gathering, for example, several elders discussed the necessity of not only including non-Tribal peoples in cultural events, but displaying indigenous symbols as a necessity for indigenous survival. Even controversial sports mascots and symbols should be tolerated, stated one elder, so long as such symbols advertise the presence of indigenous peoples, stating, "What's important is for us to be present and not stop being present." [FN3/071815]

SA: *So how do tribal youth address their personal, emotional, or mental health issues?*

TRADITIONAL HEALER: *Nowadays I think they act out more. You know, when something's wrong or they withdraw. And I think they also will seek out, maybe staying even with a relative, which was my thing. I mean, I was kind of a boarding school kid anyways. But most of the time I wasn't home because I didn't want to see, I guess, you know, my dad and what he did with his drinking and everything. So I stayed with an aunt and uncle of mine pretty much through my teen years. I was home every once and a while and stuff. So I think by targeting the youth that are at risk and showing those signs, especially with traditional things, you know, how to properly use cedar . . . or cedar, Sage, and Sweet Grass even, and the basic elements of knowing that, you know, the story behind them and teaching them that, and giving them that outlet, you know, even if the parents don't follow that way, [Tribal youth] have that somehow available to them. But most of all, getting them somewhere where they can talk, because my uncle I spent a lot of time with, I know that I could talk to him about anything, you know. So in my lifetime, I always kind of strive to be that kind of uncle and that . . . someone that our family youth can turn to and talk to if they need to. And so I think that right now it's more acting out and I think that's what kind of puts them at risk to going into gangs, and belonging to gangs and stuff is because they don't have a sense of belonging anymore. A Tribal ID card is not enough.* [PC9/102715]

Shkwaandem!

John Wayne is killing Indians again—in droves. Bang! Pow! Ping!
The bullets never touch him as he dives under the wagon.
Pow! But those Indians, those red devils sure get it.
Five years old, glued to the screen.
How ironic is this scene?
Mom says, "You know you're Indian, right?"
What? I always knew my father was darker—not like the other dads.
But he was just dad, dark or light, and what else was a dad supposed be, right?
What's Indian . . . ?
What is Indian . . . ?
What does that mean, to be Indian . . . ?

I sit in the stands, watching the dancers in the summer heat.
The drum is soft, deep, comforting, like the Earth's own heartbeat.
Bum-bum, Bum-bum . . . Those dancers sure feel it.
A teenager, glued to the scene.
How ironic it must seem.
Some people's eyes say, "You know you're white, right?"
What? I always knew that I had a lighter-skinned mother—not like some others.
But light or dark she was just mom to me. What else was she supposed to be?
What's white . . . ?
What is white . . . ?"
What does that mean, to be white . . . ?

The steam sizzles as water is thrown onto the Mishomisug,
The Grandfathers, red glowing stones settled in the pit of the lodge,
The only light in the dark interior.
Hot water splashes onto my bare skin.
Hiss . . . pop! We sing in Anishnaabekmowin
Sweat streams into the Earth.
The language I do not speak fluently, but wraps around me as heavily as the dense steam.
"Shkwaandem! Open! Open the Door Mueshka!"

"Enh. Yes." Shkwaandem—Open the door.
Like a rabbit, I shoot through the small opening, trying to escape the harsh finale of the sweat lodge—And his old hand catches my foot before I roll into the fire.

What is Indian? What is white? Questions that rise away with the steam.
Rebirthed, cast back out, anew—yet held strongly and laughingly by the old.
Not light or dark, but Ojibwa,
Anishnaabek.
What's Ojibwa?
What is Ojibwa?
What does that mean, to be Ojibwa?

. . . Where the heck did he go?

Scanning the pow-wow grounds, I finally spot my teenage nephew sitting in the stands with—surprise, surprise—a group of girls. I hustle over to the newly built pavilion to get under the shade and gulp down some water out of my bottle. I'm glad he's been making some new friends while we camped out together at the Sugar Island annual pow-wow and spiritual gathering. I ask if they know each other from school.

"No," my nephew says. "We just started talking and hanging out."

"You ever thought of getting into pow-wow dancing?" motioning to the pow-wow grounds. "I bet you'd be pretty good. You're athletic and stuff, right?"

"I don't know. I don't know anything about it," says the six-foot-one inch-tall fourteen year old.

I ask the three young ladies sitting with him how they got involved in dancing. "Did you learn in a class or did your family teach you?"

"Family. I was young and my family was into it, and so I got into it too," said one young lady.

"Isn't there a class or a group or anything that kids could get into?"

"There were classes once that were taught by an older guy at the Big Bear for a while. But a cheerleading coach or dance coach or something came over when our music was on and said, 'I don't have to listen to this, do I?'"

"You're saying a dance teacher or cheerleading coach came over and told you to turn down your music? While you were in a dance class?"

Nanabozhoo's father, Epighizhmuk, left his mother, Winona, soon after his birth. In the absence of her lover, Winona died of a broken heart. Filled with anger, Nanabozhoo traveled to the West, to the home of Epighizhmuk to confront his father. After a long journey, he arrived at the mountain home of Epighizhmuk. Nanabozhoo climbed the mountain, and upon finding his father, quickly was flooded with rage over his mother's death and his father's abandonment. A vicious battle ensued between father and son. However, Epighizhmuk, being the Spirit of the West Wind, was immortal, and Nanabozhoo, being a half-spirit, likewise could not be killed. The combat continued for a long time, with neither Nanabozhoo nor his father gaining the upper hand. Eventually, the two realized that the battle would never end, and if they continued, they would be locked in a violent struggle for eternity. Epighizhmuk presented a pipe, which they smoked as a symbol of peace and reconciliation—between father and son, past and present. Epighizhmuk gifted the Pipe to his son, Nanabozhoo, who took it home to the land of the Ojibwa. To this day, we are reminded of the clash between father and son, as thunder from the West echoes the battle that took place so long ago. Also to this day, we smoke the Pipe, and we are reminded of the power of peace and reconciliation that took place between father and son—between a conflicted past and a hopeful future.

Historical Trauma, Intergenerational Anger, and Identity

Like many indigenous peoples, Ojibwa history contains traumatic events—violent shifts in the social and natural environment, forced assimilation, racial and ethnic discrimination, forced attendance at government- and church-run boarding schools, poverty and the disastrous effects of substance abuse and preventable diseases. Over time, traumatic moments ingrained themselves within the overall history of the Sault Tribe, as family members who directly experienced such events passed their memories down, from generation to generation. Along with the description of traumatic events, however, younger generations also inherited a sense of anxiety and anger regarding these events, and perhaps an expectation of a recurrence of traumatic events.

A current example of traumatic memory surfacing within American society is when a young black man feels that he cannot trust white society, particularly white police officers, and as a result feels anxiety, stress, and perhaps anger (this is not to say that such stress and anger is not also well founded on real racist attitudes on the behalf of public institutions). The effect of traumatic memories, or the process of remembering trauma (Winter, 2008) that has taken place within an ethnic group, nationality, religious order, or gendered group can also be amplified through violent Hollywood re-creations, news coverage of past atrocities, or recurring instances of poor treatment that fulfill anticipation of trauma.

Perhaps the effect of historical trauma can explain the young girl's description of the interaction at the Big Bear Arena—a large sports complex built on the Sault Tribe reservation for Tribal members and local residents—which smacks of blunt racism. According to every interview participant, racism was a prominent issue in the past; however, racial slurs like "dirty Indian" or other such insults are far less common today. When they do surface, interviewees describe racist comments taking place as whispers within closed conversations, never said to a Tribal member's face. Tribal members or non-Tribal spouses able to pass as white are more often privy to incendiary remarks due to their "non-Indian" appearance—a situation described by several interviewees as highly awkward for the commentator.

If racism is less common in the Eastern Upper Peninsula, at least toward Tribal members, did the young girl simply imagine a brazen insult? Staff members at the Big Bear Arena describe conflicts, racial or otherwise, with young people as unusual, and during participant-observation, zero instances of conflict or discrimination were documented. Yet, the young lady spoke with conviction. Mentioning the story to a school counselor led to a key insight:

> Those kids, if they're raised by their grandparents, they're carrying that old anger, that generational anger. Kids that have never even

> experienced anything like that will talk about the boarding school days. Those aren't their words. That's not their anger that they're carrying.
>
> [PC5I1/081215]

Is it possible, then, that the young woman at the pow-wow is not simply acknowledging a traumatic ethnic history, but allowing the events of the past, as told by family, community, and popular representations of history, to bend her perception of present circumstances? Are Ojibwa youth, inheriting an intergenerational anger, responding emotionally to imagined labels ("dirty Indians") and events not experienced ("boarding school days") with an anger "that is not theirs"?

Expressions of Indianness, Traditional and Non-Traditional

Further frustrating efforts to revitalize Ojibwa knowledge, practice, and values, however, is a conflict revolving around what values are 'traditional,' and what values and practices are 'non-traditional'—or in some cases, stereotypical or Pan-Indian—notions of Indianness. Describing this conflict requires a short elaboration on what is 'traditional.' Many Bowheting Ojibwa use the term 'traditional,' to give the sense that a person, group, object, event, or process is 'in line' with Ojibwa cultural norms, or is authentic to and represents a continuation of practices and values that are expressive of Ojibwa culture. 'Traditional' may also support a false sense of timelessness, or an image of Ojibwa culture (and indigenous culture more generally) as essentially unaffected. This sense of timelessness, however, does not exist in any cultural reality, as societies change with the passage of time and must respond to constantly shifting social and natural environments.

Observed over short periods, a river shows little or no change—leading one to believe that the river is the same as it always was and will remain true to its current depths, bends, and other traits. In truth, each day that the river flows, the depths, bends, and direction of the river change, however unnoticed. Likewise, the individual who traverses the river changes with each crossing. As the ancient Greek philosopher Heraclitus stated:

> No man ever steps in the same river twice, for it's not the same river and he's not the same man.

Culture acts similarly, shifting constantly with time and the progression of events, however minuscule those changes may seem in a single lifetime. Similar to the situation where one cannot step in the same river twice, one cannot judge a culture or ethnic group to be the same 'as it was' at any point in the past. A false sense of timelessness or constancy, however, can, has, and continues to distort the image of specific sections of Tribal societies as unchanging or true to 'traditional,' timeless practices, and other sections of Tribal societies as 'non-traditional' and modern. Traditions, however, are exercises in remembering a common past, and the events, places, practices, and values are historically shared by a specific group of people. The purposes and limits of traditions, however, may be lost to 'traditionalists' who assert their authenticity in re-creating Tribal practices. More appropriate, non-competitive terms must be used to describe observable actions and expressions of cultural attitudes, beliefs, and values, such as *customs* (Ann Miles, Ph.D Western Michigan University, personal communication, 2015) or *practices*.

The word 'traditional' continues to carry a particular connotation for Sault Tribe members, and Native American and First Nations peoples more generally. Practices, objects, events, and processes are labeled as 'traditional' if they are seen as representative of pre-colonial indigenous lifestyle (i.e., religion, dress, language, economic systems, and food ways). Therefore, the terms 'traditional' and 'non-traditional' (or modern) represent a non-Western (indigenous, Tribal) vs Western (Euro-American, colonizer) dichotomy. No matter the origins, the conflict between 'traditional' and 'non-traditional' is perpetuated and expressed within the indigenous community itself, often in the form of stereotypical representation of "Indianness" or imagery of the "stereotypical Indian" (Berkhofer, 1978).

The application and adoption of the stereotypical Indian in the Sault Tribe is visible in the form of popular imagery posted in residential areas, Tribal buildings, and Tribal-associated locations. Images vary from the romantic "Noble Savage," wearing a flowing feathered bonnet and fighting the march of Western civilization from horseback (Images 4, 5) to the Native American who is inherently capable of ethereal, mystic communication with the moon, stars, planets, and the animals of the Earth (Images 1, 6). Compare such imagery with the fishing and canoeing—not horseback riding—activities of the Ojibwa, or the relatively high conversion of Bowheting Ojibwa, leading to intertwined, syncretic religious beliefs including aspects of Christianity and Ojibwa spirituality. The back and forth confusion over what it is to be Ojibwa is humorously and pointedly echoed in the film *Smoke Signals* (1998), as the main characters go back and forth on "how to be a Real Indian" and the importance of being "stoic":

VICTOR JOSEPH: You gotta look mean or people won't respect you. White people will run all over you if you don't look mean. You gotta look like a warrior! You gotta look like you just came back from killing a buffalo!

THOMAS BUILDS-THE-FIRE: But our tribe never hunted buffalo—we were fishermen.

VICTOR JOSEPH: What! You want to look like you just came back from catching a fish? This ain't "Dances with Salmon" you know!

In the Sault Tribe, individuals who are searching for their Ojibwa identity or have a desire to learn more of their Ojibwa traditions may move toward the imagined ideas of the Hollywood Indian that are so popular on the national scene, rather than participate in activities or base their search on an activity, object, or place specific to Ojibwa culture. The 'stereotypical' or Hollywood Indian, therefore, may confuse any attempt to create a thriving, unique sense of Ojibwa culture.

Native Americans, however, did not simply accept a "white man's" idea of what it is to be Indian, a conclusion explained in the acclaimed documentary *Reel Injuns: On the Trail of the Hollywood Indian* (2009). *Real Injuns* powerfully displays the history and impact of stereotyped imagery of Indians in film and still pictures, media expanding white Euro-Americans' previous and ongoing obsession with the "other" ("other" being strange, exotic, savage, uncivilized, and at times sexually eroticized peoples of the colored, non-Western world). Rather than be definitively portrayed as living stereotypes and ingested into the history of mainstream America, indigenous peoples manipulated their growing popularity to carve out a unique, if altered, identity.

Likewise, observations of Sault Tribe members and Ojibwa from nearby bands go against the claim that Native Americans are simply taking on the image of the "White Man's Indian." Turning over handmade pieces of art, clothing items, and accessories, for example, show what could be considered patriotic American symbols being adapted to fit 'Native' themes (e.g., traditional jewelry made with American coins (usually buffalo head nickels), chokers embedded with coinage or patriotic symbols, hats that boldly claim on the front "Native Veteran" and the branch of service and conflict). The adaptation of items not designed for Native themed artwork or clothing speaks to the indigenous people's ability to demand, accumulate, and use American items and symbols to fulfill their cultural tastes as they see fit.

Adapting Euro-American products to meet indigenous purposes has a long precedent, especially in the history of the fur trade. Since the beginning of indigenous and European interaction, Anishinaabek and other indigenous groups adapted European trade goods to fit indigenous forms of art and style. Items traded in the seventeenth and eighteenth centuries, particularly brass and metal-based items, provide examples of such adaptations. For example, the Anishnaabek realized that sewing thimbles in a line onto shirts and garments produced a 'tinkling sound,' as a person moved or danced. The Anishnaabek also used strips of copper, rolled into a cone shape, for this purpose. "Tinkling cones," as they are often called, adorned shirts and dresses, replacing or accompanying existing forms of rattles that provided musical accompaniment and ornamentation. Reflecting on indigenous adaptation of trade goods to fit within existing cultural contexts and needs caused archaeologists and historians to question an earlier presumption that trade in and use of Western items indicated an acculturation of indigenous peoples to Western society (Nassaney, 2015: chapter 4). The Ojibwa and many indigenous peoples continue to sew handmade and factory-produced versions of the tinkling cone, bells, and hoof-rattles onto "jingle dresses" and other pow-wow regalia.

Another example of Ojibwa people appropriating non-Native items and symbols takes place during the flag or color guard ceremony, which is a central, public event of pow-wows and spiritual gatherings. Tribal and in many cases non-Tribal military veterans carry national, Tribal, clan-directional, and military service flags, as well as any eagle feather staff present, in a basic formation around the pow-wow grounds at the beginning and conclusion of a pow-wow. Eagle staffs, adorned with eagle feathers, sacred symbols to Anishnaabek and many Eastern Woodlands Tribes, are traditional versions of flags or symbols of the Ojibwa community. While the American flag is front and center in the formation during this event, veterans hold all symbols, including the American flag, at the same elevation and angle during the honor song, an equivalent to a national anthem.

The significance of carrying the American flag at the same height as other flags becomes apparent when comparing to non-Tribal military or civilian color guard ceremonies, where the color guard holds the American flag at a higher elevation and angle during the national anthem, signifying the preeminence of the national flag. Although it is doubtful that Ojibwa veterans purposefully practice improper flag etiquette in any other way (for instance, always preventing flags and eagle feathers from touching the ground) or re-create the Tribal version of 'colors,' the military term for raising or retiring organizational flags, this treatment of the American flag is accepted by Tribal society. The neutral treatment of the American flag as a symbol may be due to a belief that the American symbol of sovereignty is not above or below the Ojibwa eagle staff or Tribal flag in terms of loyalty or ethnic symbolism. Equal elevation of the American flag may represent a hierarchy of political-ethnic symbols; marking out national identity (i.e., American citizenship) as an addition to, as opposed to a replacement of, Anishnaabek concepts of political-ethnic identity.

According to many elders and traditional healers, responsibility, dedication to the community, and the passing on of Ojibwa values are central to a stable sense of identity. Indeed, the passing on of common values and responsibilities is central to any ethnic group's shared identity. Sault Tribe members often point to forced assimilation, socioeconomic stressors, addiction and substance abuse, and related behavioral issues to explain the loss of Ojibwa identity and traditional values. However, what it means to be Ojibwa—or Chippewa, Native American, American, a card-carrying Sault Tribe member, fake Indian, a quarter, half, or full blood—represents a revolving door of ethnic, official, and stereotyped identities that influences the strength and nature of one's connection with indigenous culture, and more broadly, one's sense of self and purpose.

Despite such strong examples of including symbols and practices from so-called dominant American society, the stereotypical Indian imagery remains strong and threatens to undermine Ojibwa identity. Many community members meet stereotyped and other forms of 'Indian' identity with self-criticism, self-awareness, and of course, humor. Elders are especially thoughtful regarding 'Indian' identity, which they have seen develop amongst their children and grandchildren. As I sat with a core group of elders at the Sugar Island Pow-Wow and Spiritual Gathering, the subject of how elders viewed themselves, and how they are treated with a glowing sense of reverence (Figure 2; pun intended), was treated with sharp humor. One elder suggested that they should "bottle our sweat and sell it" as an elixir: "Come and get it! Guaranteed 100 percent pure Indian sweat. Cures anything."

Works Cited

Angell, Kurz, and Gottfried (1998) "Suicide and North American Indians: A Social Constructivist Perspective." *Journal of Multicultural Social Work*. 6 (3–4), 1–26.

Bardill, J. (n.d.) "Tribal Sovereignty and Enrollment Determinations." *National Congress of American Indians*. Accessed August 29, 2017. http://genetics.ncai.org/tribal-sovereignty-and-enrollment-determinations.cfm

Barlow, A., Tingey, L., Cwik, M., Goklish, N., Larzelere-Hinton, F., Lee, A., Suttle, R., Mullany, B., and Walkup, J. T. (2012) "Understanding the Relationship Between Substance Use and Self-Injury in American Indian Youth." *The American Journal of Drug and Alcohol Abuse*. 38 (5), 403.

Berkhofer, R. F. (1978) *The White Man's Indian: Images of the American Indian From Columbus to the Present*. New York: Knopf.

Broad, G., Boyer, S., and Chataway C. (2006) "We Are Still the Aniishnaabe Nation: Embracing Culture and Identity in Batchewana First Nation." *Canadian Journal of Communication*. 31 (1), 35–58.

Cleland, C. E. (1992) *Rites of Conquest: The History and Culture of Michigan's Native Americans*. University of Michigan Press.

Cleland, C. E. (2001) *The Place of the Pike (Gnoozhekaaning): A History of the Bay Mills Indian Community*. University of Michigan Press.

Dressler, W., and Bindon, J. (2000) "The Health Consequences of Cultural Consonance: Cultural Dimensions of Lifestyle, Social Support and Arterial Blood

Pressure in an African American Community." *American Anthropologist*. 102 (2), 244–260.

Goodkind, J., Ross-Toledo, R., John, K., Hall, S., Ross, J., Freeland, L., Coletta, L., Becenti-Fundark, L., Poola, E., Begay-Roanhorse, T., and Lee, C. (2010) "Promoting Healing and Restoring Trust: Policy Recommendations for Improving Behavioral Health Care for American Indian/Alaska Native Adolescents." *American Journal of Community Psychology*. 46 (3), 386–394.

Jackson, D. (2002) *Our Elders Lived It: American Indian Identity in the City*. DeKalb: Northern Illinois University Press.

Nassaney, M. (2015). The archaeology of the North American fur trade. (American experience in archaeological perspective). Gainesville, University of Florida Press.

Niezen, R. (2015) "The Durkheim-Tarde Debate and the Social Study of Aboriginal Youth Suicide." *Transcultural Psychiatry*. 52 (1), 96–114.

Peschel, K. (2006) *Keewaydinoquay: Stories From My Youth*. Ann Arbor: University of Michigan Press.

Smoke signals / a Shadowcatcher Entertainment production; directed by Chris Eyre; screenplay by Sherman Alexie; produced by Scott Rosenfelt, Larry Estes. United States: Miramax Films; Burbank, CA: Miramax Home Entertainment 2000.

Teeple, B. and Kamuda A. (1994) *Kitchigamic Anishinabeg: The People of the Great Lakes*. Sault Ste Marie Tribe of Chippewa Indians.

Walls, M., Hautala, D., and Hurley, J. (2014) "'Rebuilding Our Community': Hearing Silenced Voices on Aboriginal Youth Suicide." *Transcultural Psychiatry*. 51 (1), 47–72.

Winter, J. (2008). *Remembering War The Great War between Memory and History in the 20th Century*. Yale University Press.

Figure 3.1 Praying/Meditating Indian poster (re-used with permission of the Native American Student Center, Lake Superior State University)

Figure 3.2 Walking Elder, Mystical Elder poster (re-used with permission of the Native American Student Center, Lake Superior State University)

Figure 3.3 Masked Indigenous Person painting/print (re-used with permission of the Native American Student Center, Lake Superior State University)

Figure 3.4 Plains Indian on Horse painting/print (re-used with permission of the Native American Student Center, Lake Superior State University)

Figure 3.5 Plains Indian with Rifle statue (re-used with permission of the Native American Student Center, Lake Superior State University)

Figure 3.6 Female Indian with Animals by Riverside, Elders or Ancestors in Background painting/sketch (re-used with permission of the Native American Student Center, Lake Superior State University)

During an extremely harsh winter, a hunter became desperate to provide for his starving family. With no strength to chase game, he went to a shaman that was known to be powerful. He begged the Shaman to give him a medicine that would allow him to hunt. The Shaman gave him a medicine, which he was instructed to take. The hunter went to the forest, took the medicine, and soon fell into a deep sleep. When the hunter awoke, he found that he had amazing strength and speed and grew larger than any man. He also felt a great hunger. Stalking through the forest in search of game, he came upon a village of animals—beaver, otter, squirrel, deer, and many other types. His mouth watering, he broke out of the brush and began snatching and eating the animals. His belly stretched to its limits, but the more he ate the hungrier he became. Only after he devoured the animals did he realize that it was not a village of animals, but of people. Howling with grief, but with a hunger that was still not sated, he tore off into the forest. What the hunter became was a Weendigo, a monstrosity that fed on human flesh and could never be full no matter how much it ate.

Crap, I'm late.

I just received a call about a meeting on substance abuse prevention—that started ten minutes ago. I might be able to take some notes on the discussion if the pickup in front of me sporting Red Wings stickers on the rear window would get out of the way. After several hundred yards of painstaking slowness, the truck turns left toward the Big Bear and I speed ahead for five hundred feet before hanging a right into the eastern casino entrance, park my truck and jump out, notebook in hand. I eventually find the "Whitefish Room" in the lower level. Each conference room in the casino complex is named after some type of local fish or geographical feature. Did they name this conference room after the delicious whitefish or Whitefish Point? I'm not exactly sure. I silently push through the ADHD moment and the double doors into the dim interior. Knowing that the meeting is in full swing, I enter tentatively like the party crasher that I am, and thankfully I am waved over by one of the council members who invited me to participate as an observer. I wave back and slip along the wall on the left side of the room toward the open seat next to her.

Everyone is seated at the U-shaped configuration of long tables near the front of the large, roughly fifty foot wide and one hundred foot long conference room. The open end of the "U" is dominated by the soft glow of a projection screen.

I start taking frantic notes as soon as my butt hits the seat, despite several eyes that seem to say "who the heck are you and what are you doing here?" My host leans over and says "I can never make all of these meetings, but I try. You can't make it to everything."

I reply with a nod and smile, and whisper back "I understand."

The conversation continued hardly abated by my minor disruption.

"What's the plan . . . ?"

"What's the strategy here . . . ?"

"How is this going to work . . . ?"

General questions and dizzying acronyms fly back and forth between the nearly two dozen people assigned to attend the meeting or who voluntarily showed up to give their input. Among them are various representatives and department heads from the service areas of the Sault Tribe. I try to take notes, but it's about as impossible as snatching the words out of the air with my bare hands. About two minutes into it, I do the same thing that I do when a professor goes off on a rant, and I set the notebook on the table and simply listen while jotting down periodic highlights.

Today's meeting takes place between members of the TAP committee, or the committee in charge of the implementing Tribal Action Plan, which is a Department of Justice funded program that was formed in response to destructive issues in the Sault Tribe community, mainly focusing on substance abuse. As I walked in, the committee was discussing the data from two surveys that were completed in support of the TAP mission. The surveys included focus groups and community meetings where Tribal members could voice concerns over substance abuse.

"So what should we do with this data?" a young woman poses to the rest of the group. "It's not translatable. We need to understand how to take the data and use it in our departments."

The young woman who was acting as a presenter or moderator of sorts echoed the sentiment, commenting on the "language barrier" that exists between the "foreign language" of the data and how it is supposed to be included directly in the various divisions within the Sault Tribe.

The committee seemed to be working on some type of flowchart, beginning with the data from focus groups, interviews, and surveys to coordinators and department heads, and finally to the workers and specialists from different departments. Reports from the lower level specialists, according to the conversation, would then be kicked back to the Board of Directors as well as other action plan committees. Yet, listening in on the discussion it seems unclear that there is any collective understanding of the flowchart of information, how the reporting process would work, or how information would be included in policies and procedures.

Before I could finish that thought, a young man sitting farther to my right, in an attempt to clarify the use of data and the overall responsibilities of the TAP, said, "but that's what the project coordinator's responsibility is."

"But the data on the west side of the seven county service area is going to be different from the data on the east," chimes in a middle aged woman sitting across and to the right of me.

"Yes, every community is different," replied a Tribal Health clinic administrator, who was getting visibly exasperated at the level of confusion.

This launched the group into a mini-discussion around the fact that the data overall does not represent the individual communities' concerns, especially the challenges that the rural villages face. Without transportation, how would people access drug rehab or counseling?

Just when that conversation was coming to an end, an elderly man to my right questioned how the planning process will prioritize certain challenges, asking, "Has anyone thought of that?"

While agreeing with that point, a clinic administrator impressed upon the group the social action aspect of the plan. With a light bang on the table to accentuate his point, he says, "we don't just want to find out what's wrong, we want solutions."

The meeting started winding down, with an eye towards scheduling future meeting dates, with several people emphasizing the need for dates and times that are more available. An attempt was made to pass out "homework" to various representatives, to be completed before the next meeting; to which a young woman with dark hair replied through a chuckle, "What, specifically, is this homework?"

Several others chuckled along as they folded up notebooks and powered down computers, leaving the question hanging in the air.

I made my way over to one of the more outspoken committee members whom I'd talked to previously and asked if she could fill me in on her thoughts on the TAP meeting and the parts I missed. "Sure, just let me grab my bags real quick so we can step out for a smoke."

Making our way out the double doors and just out of earshot of the committee members, she proclaimed, more to herself than to me, "That was a crap shoot." Obviously, she was not very pleased with the results of the meeting. Several people followed us out into the atrium who were either leaving for their respective offices or coming out to appease their habit in the comfort of the air-conditioned atrium (smoking is allowed in the casino).

I was introduced to a person from the Sault Tribe justice building, whose presence is supposed to ensure the TAP was implemented according to federal regulations. Funding by the Department of Justice comes with the stipulation that the recipient follow guidelines of the Tribal Law and Order Act of 2010 throughout the planning and objective stages. After asking what the "end result" of the meeting process is supposed to be, [XXXX] said the program is meant to install a "wrap-around approach" to substance abuse and related issues. Basically, the Department of Justice, Anishnaabek Child and Family Services, the Health Department, Tribal police, and other administrative arms would unify under a single network or model and shared approach to substance abuse.

After talking a bit more, [XXXX] stubbed out her cigarette. Even though the meeting was over, she said, it's good to make sure you wrap things up with people who are clustered afterwards, discussing things here and there. With that, we walked back in and I took the opportunity to introduce myself to some of the other TAP members.

I said hello to several people, and ended up talking with [XXXX] from [XXXX]. Still confused about the structure of the TAP committee and its purpose, I asked him to explain. I also asked how he feels about the development of youth suicide or the meaning of youth suicide for the community.

"As it relates to this?" he asked.

"Sure," I replied.

Using 'the pot of gold at the end of the rainbow' as a metaphor, he described the nuances of the TAP meeting and committee structure. Meetings, he said, are places to look for possible funding, a watering hole of sorts where people of various backgrounds gather to find resources for social services and institutions for the betterment of the community. He added, with a bit of regret, "There's a lot of conflict and competition for this pot of gold which can make the flow of resources into a trickle."

In an effort to sum up his thoughts on the effects of competition between departments, and the trickle-down process resulting from organizational bureaucracy and the ineffectiveness of fixed budgeting systems, he concluded: "I guess that's the cost of civilization." [FN38/072215]

As long as we had funding, and people knew we had funding, there was a lot of support for that program and we were able to do a lot in the community. As soon as they found out that the funding was gone . . . we went from having like thirty people at the board meeting, until at the end it was just like two people. So a lot of people got that idea that we need that money, but really there was still a lot of things we could do without money. We could have those, ah, even though talking circles were not traditional for our communities, Ojibwa communities, it's something people accept. So we could have more of those ceremonies. We could have talked to the kids and with the parents about these problems and it doesn't really cost any money. Seems like as soon as we didn't have the funding we lost the support. And then talking about funding, you know, I know our Tribes are stretched with . . . as far as money is . . . you know, there still coulda been more support for the [XXXX] program. You know, we kinda forget about . . . we seem to worry more about casinos and how they're operating than we do about our own people. [PC00/011314]

"Listen, I want to tell you something else. And you have to promise you'll never repeat it."

"Okay," I said.

"Promise me."

"Okay, okay, I promise I won't repeat it."

"Not to anyone. Not even your parents."

"Nobody."

"Okay, then," he said and leaned closer to me because he didn't even want the trees to hear what he was going to say. "You have to leave this reservation."

"I'm going to Spokane with my data later."

"No, I mean you have to leave the rez forever."

"What do you mean?"

"You were right to throw that book at me. I deserved to get smashed in the face for what I've done to Indians. Every white person on this rez should get smashed in the face. But, let me tell you this. All the Indians should get smashed in the face, too."

I was shocked. Mr. P was furious.

"The only thing you kids are being taught is how to give up. Your friend Rowdy, he's given up. That's why he likes to hurt people. He wants them to feel as bad as he does."

"He doesn't hurt me."

"He doesn't hurt you because you're the only good thing in his life. He doesn't want to give that up. It's the only thing he hasn't given up."

Mr. P grabbed me by the shoulders and leaned so close to me that I could smell his breath.

Onions and garlic and hamburger and shame and pain.

"All these kids have given up," he said. "All your friends. All the bullies. And their mothers and fathers have given up, too. And their grandparents gave up and their grandparents before them. And me and every other teacher here. We're all defeated."

Mr. P was crying.

I couldn't believe it.

I'd never seen a sober adult cry.

"But not you," Mr. P said. "You can't give up. You won't give up. You threw that book in my face because somewhere inside, you refuse to give up."

I didn't know what he was talking about. Or maybe I just didn't want to know.

Jeez, it was a lot of pressure to put on a kid. I was carrying the burden of my race, you know? I was going to get a bad back from it.

"If you stay on this rez," Mr. P said, "they're going to kill you. I'm going to kill you. We're all going to kill you. You can't fight us forever."

"I don't want to fight anybody," I said.

"You've been fighting since you were born," he said. "You fought off that brain surgery. You fought off those seizures. You fought off all the drunks and drug addicts. You kept your hope. And now, you have to take your hope and go somewhere where other people have hope."

I was starting to understand. He was a math teacher. I had to add my hope to somebody else's hope. I had to multiply hope by hope.

"Where is hope?" I asked. "Who has hope?"

"Son," Mr. P said. "You're going to find more and more hope the farther and farther you walk away from this sad, sad, sad reservation."

4 Hopelessness Kills

Development of Risk Factors for Youth Suicide and Barriers to Treatment and Relief

SA: *How would you describe those who are most at risk for suicide in the Sault Tribe community?*

ADMINISTRATOR: *The people that don't have a lot of options. They don't think they have a lot of options in life. And they don't have a lot of hope in their life. Hope for the future.*

—Sault Tribe Health Center Administrator [PC131/71615]

In the late 1960s, American psychologist Martin Seligman used canines to test the concept of *learned helplessness*. The first phase of his experiments involved placing a dog in a box-like compartment divided in the center by a low fence. The side of the fence where the dog stood produced an electric shock through the floor. When the experimenters administered the shock, the dog did what you would expect it to do—it eventually jumped over the low fence to the other side. As the experiment repeated, the dog took less time to escape (Overmier and Seligman, 1967; Seligman, 1972).

During the next phase of the experiment, however, researchers restrained the dog in a harness that prevented escape from the electric shock. The dog responded to the shock by attempting to escape and kicking, biting, and pulling at the harness. After repeated shocks, the dog learned that no matter what actions it took there could be no escape or relief from the pain. Ultimately, the dog stopped trying to escape altogether and settled into a state of depression and anxiety.

The final phase tested the experiment's hypothesis, which posited that the dog, released from the harness, would not attempt to escape when the experimenters initiated electric shock through the floor. As hypothesized, rather than jump over the fence, the dog stayed in place and endured the shock. Due to the inability to escape electric shock on numerous occasions, Seligman and his peers surmised, the dog settled into a depressive state and learned to accept a state of helplessness.

Previous sections discussed the erosion of a solid sense of identity and purpose, and the potential weakening of resilience as a result, which, combined with risk factors (e.g., substance abuse in family, mental health disorders, dysfunctional family relationships, lack of economic opportunity), contribute to suicide ideation and self-harm (e.g., Herne, Bartholomew and Weahkee, 2014; Olson and Wahab, 2006). This section explores the potential role of hopelessness—or learned helplessness—as a culminating force behind the ongoing rash of suicides in indigenous communities. Viewed as a process, the development of hopelessness resembles a cycle. Youth, consistently exposed to various risk factors in the social environment and choosing to adopt unhealthy coping mechanisms (e.g., substance abuse; Herring, 1994), may feel that certain pains, environments, or habits of lifestyle are inescapable. Accepting harmful environments and negative coping mechanisms as a status quo eventually normalizes psychologically and socioeconomically degrading conditions. Unlike most animals, however, human beings have the wherewithal to escape such destructive cycles by choosing a final option. Risk factors for youth suicide in the Sault Tribe, as described by interview participants, follow common themes, specifically:

- Availability and use of drugs and alcohol, especially prescription drugs
- Lack of economic opportunities or healthy activities for youth and young adults
- Dysfunctional family settings and a lack of available family for emotional support
- Previous or ongoing sexual, physical, or emotional abuse
- Absence of identity or a sense of identity and purpose
- Bullying in schools (emotional abuse)
- Stress from “coming out” or having “come out” as gay or lesbian
- Inadequate mental health care, lack of psychiatric services
- Fearful of stigma, specifically fearful of being viewed as “crazy” or being seen seeking help
- Not knowledgeable of traditional teachings on health, death, and suicide
- Replacement of interpersonal interaction with virtual interaction
- Lack of resilience or inability to process emotional discomfort and painful life events
- Availability of firearms and other materials that could be used for self-harm

The RAPID Assessment for Adolescent Services survey, which the Sault Area High School administers annually to sophomore and junior grade students, provides a quantitative measurement of exposure to at-risk factors and engagement in risk behaviors. Specifically, questions gauge students’ reactions to anger, the availability of adult help, frequency of suicidal thoughts or attempts, presence of depression, engagement in sexual behavior, drug use/abuse, alcohol use/abuse, cigarette use, use/carrying of weapons, physical/sexual abuse, bullying, use of safety equipment, physical exercise, healthy diet, and approaches to weight loss ("vomiting, laxatives, starving yourself?").

Between 2009 and 2016, the RAPID Assessment results indicated that American Indian students' answered positively to engagement in at-risk behaviors at higher rates than did their white/Caucasian counterparts in nearly every category. Specifically, the overall American Indian population (23.8 percent of the student body) is overrepresented at 25–36 percent of the total at-risk population (depending on category). In contrast, the white/Caucasian population (73 percent of the total student population) is underrepresented in the at-risk population at 59–69 percent. The only area in which American Indian students showed a low risk was in response to the question "Do you have at least one adult in your life that you can talk to about any problems or worries?" Having a high number of adults to speak to is not surprising given the extended family dynamic in American Indian cultures.

The psychological harm caused by exposure to risk factors is of concern to Tribal and non-Tribal residents of the Eastern Upper Peninsula alike. That being said, Ojibwa (and indigenous youth generally) may be more vulnerable to increases in risk factors by simple virtue of belonging to an ethnic group deeply affected by the consequential damages of a colonial relationship.

As previously discussed, most studies on youth suicide in Native American communities are quantitative and largely focus on identifying the risk factors and risk behaviors of individuals. Statistical conclusions, however, minus a contextual understanding of ethnic history and society threaten to color specific groups as at-risk while failing to highlight the development of unhealthy environments. Furthermore, the language used by social scientists, policymakers, and mental health organizations inadvertently correlate 'at-risk' with 'indigenous,' 'individual,' and 'youth,' effectively constructing an additional sense of identity—the 'at-risk identity.' In effect, simply advertising a high suicide rate and above-average risk exposure provides negligible comprehension of the development of risk behavior and risk factors within the environment.

Approaching the suicidal person and suicide as a behavior biographically can facilitate such comprehension. The framework and a significant number of interview questions are devoted to such a biographical understanding, resulting in direct descriptions of suicidal persons, their lifestyle, choices, identity, and the challenges and barriers to treatment. As a result, many of the risks encountered in this study originate not from the at-risk individual, but from the barriers that stand between individuals seeking or requiring treatment, or desiring healthier lifestyles, and the resources that may prevent or protect against suicidal ideation.

The above summary regarding risk for youth suicide in the Sault Tribe community leaves much room for future discussion and research. The majority of this work, however, pivots to the social, economic, and historical factors found in Ojibwa communities that may contribute to behavioral health risks and youth suicide, barriers to mental health care, and achievement of social, mental, and spiritual health and areas of strength and resilience within the community.

The weakening of the family unit can be especially devastating to an Ojibwa child's sense of safety, security, and self-worth, largely due to the importance of family, particularly the extended family unit, as a central institution of Ojibwa culture. Charles Cleland describes family as composed of "father, mother, children, and perhaps an attached grandparent or unmarried brother or sister" (1992). "This group," he says:

> is the minimal working unit of Anishnabeg society because its members possess the knowledge, time, energy, and skill needed to perform all the tasks required for survival. These tasks are assigned, by custom, according to sex and age. For example, men are responsible for hunting, women for cooking and making clothes, children for collecting wood, and grandparents for education, and on and on. This division of labor within the family is vital for survival, because no person alone could hope to know enough and do enough to stay alive. All people are, therefore, members of the family at all times. There is no escape from the family.
>
> (Cleland, 1992: 44)

While Cleland's description is that of eighteenth- and nineteenth-century Ojibwa family life, modern, twentieth-century Ojibwa culture continues to exhibit extended family structure. Cross-generational relationships between grandparents and grandchildren, for instance, continue to be a mainstay of Ojibwa family structure. Elders were responsible for providing an informal education and advice and guidance to youth, especially during emotionally charged events, such as puberty. In her 1930s study of Ojibwa communities, anthropologist Inez Hilger states:

> A Chippewa child was not subjected to formal education, such as we conceive it, but it was taught in an informal way to conform to the moral standards, as well as to the religious, the economic, and the political pattern of his tribe. It learnt, too, the mental content of the culture pattern of its people and participated in their diversions. Much of this knowledge was learned by boys and girls before they reached puberty; all of it was expected to be theirs before marriage. . . .

> Methods employed in training children were those of lecturing and counseling, of listening in, and of having ideals presented; of *imitation of elders in play or of participation with them in serious work and ceremonials . . .*
>
> *Although parents did much toward training their own children, they were quite willing that grandparents should take upon themselves a goodly share of the responsibility of doing so. Grandparents not only instructed children by word of mouth, but taught them by demonstrating to them in participating in the daily routine of work.*
>
> (Hilger, 56–57; italics added)

Grandparents, as well as aunts, uncles, and grandparents, continue to fill the role of surrogate or non-biological primary parents for children—a role filled out by economic necessity and supported by cultural design. Uncle, for instance, directly translated from Anishnaabemowin to English is "father" (Personal communication with John Haskell, 2010). While adoptive relationships may provide food, shelter, child rearing, and basic emotional support, Ojibwa adoptive relationships may take place outside of conventional standards and practices for adoption. Adoptive relationships can take place during or after adulthood and rely on recognition of social, emotional, and spiritual needs of the adoptee and adopter. It is common to hear youth, adults, and elders refer to themselves, or to others, as "my son," "father," "cousin," or "our child," without any biological relationship existing between the parties.

One example of an adoptive relationship took place while I was sitting with Father John Haskell at the Sugar Island Pow-Wow and Spiritual Gathering (though he often prefers "Brother" to the honorific of Father). Brother John, a well-loved Elder and Catholic priest at Saint Isaac Jogues Church in Sault Sainte Marie, is considered by many a man of wide knowledge of Ojibwa and other forms of spirituality. During our sit-down, he commented to a woman elder, whom he referred to as his "sister," about how proud he was of their "son," gesturing to a man in his thirties who was then dancing. While scandal over the celibacy of priests would not be news to history, to suggest a biological parenting would cause great laughter. After listening to more conversation, it also became clear that his "sister" was not a biological sibling. Recognizing the need for spiritual guidance and emotional support for the young man, at some point in the young man's youth Brother John and his sister provided guidance for the now-adult man.

Adoptive relationships and the need to keep children with Tribal communities has also been recognized by Sault Tribe Anishnaabek Children and Family Services, which made it a policy to place Tribal children, whenever possible, with extended family and non-biological adoptive parents from the Tribal community. Even outside of biological or adoptive relationships, however, adults and older children often treat the very young with a strong, automatic familiarity and care. The following anecdote involving my own son at a local event in the Bay Mills Indian Community, a neighboring Anishnaabek community, bears this out:

> For the hundredth time, I ask my son to calm down. I must keep a constant eye on him as we shuffle forward in the dinner line in the Bay Mills Indian Community YMCA gymnasium. That evening the Bay Mills Tribe put on a mixed cultural event at the "Y," with a Korean dance group performing traditional song and dance alongside a home drum group. The food ahead represents the multi-cultural atmosphere. Locally caught white fish, salads, and fry bread are placed buffet style alongside Korean foods like fried seaweed, noodle based dishes, and a traditional Korean tea.
>
> Just when I think I might have to take him outside to calm down, a middle-aged woman in a long skirt behind us exclaims "Aren't you cute?!," and scoops him up, placing him on the vacant side of her hip—the other side being occupied with her one year old. The movement was so natural that Liam didn't hesitate for a moment in taking in her and the husband's adoration, quickly manipulating them into further praise with his smiles and laughter (something he excels at).
>
> This was a bit shocking at first, having met neither of the parents (though as it turns out I'd spoken before with the father, who is a member of the local drum group and an instructor at nearby Bay Mills Community College). Anyone looking would assume that we were all family, or perhaps if they had not seen me with Liam earlier, that he was their child.
>
> [FN00/070015]

Lacking the circle of social, economic, spiritual and emotional support of biological and adoptive relationships, however, interviewees believe, raises a child's risk for suicidal ideation. Highlighting the need for social circles of support, a cultural program specialist, who often works with youth, describes at-risk youth as:

> [t]he ones who don't have anybody to turn to. The ones who have no resources. And by resources, I mean parents who they can speak with. Some kids don't feel comfortable about speaking with their parents about different things. Some don't have parents they can talk to, but some have maybe an auntie or a cousin maybe . . .
>
> [PC6/072315]

Conversely, family can also turn from a source of strength to a direct cause for anxiety and low self-esteem amongst youth. A Sault Area Schools counselor describes how parents and surrounding adults can pressure students to inherit an attitude or mentality of helplessness and an acceptance of present circumstances:

> I had parents tell me 'my life is good enough for my kids. They don't need to be better than me.' So that aspect of the parents are going to hold the children down, and overcoming that level where it's okay to live off assistance. And I'm not saying anything's wrong with subsidized housing, it definitely is needed. But that lack of striving to . . . overcome that, and to do better and want better for your children—I think that's a major blockage that we need to get past in the tribal community. Because some of our . . . they're not even elders, but some of the parents, they didn't have any better. They came from the same thing, [so] why should their children want more? It's overcoming that, and that's what frustrates me is that mindset. That what I have is good enough. You should want more for your children. . . .
>
> [PC5/081215]

A former Juvenile Probation officer also observed "recidivism" (relapse into criminal behavior) or a "revolving door" of criminal activity, substance abuse, physical/sexual abuse, and neglect in families that begins with parents and continues with Tribal children:

> A lot of it [the risk factors] has, in my opinion, to [do with] the economic aspects of tribal youth that are living within our reservations. Some of them are living in poverty levels. Their parents are unemployed so there's lack of income. Substance abuse that is rampant. Also the incarceration and most of these kids coming from a single-family home. The parents are either divorced or one of the parents is incarcerated, which is that whole social history that has followed them. And when I worked at the court I said this all the time, it is a revolving door. We get the same kids. And the kids that I had, their parents were in before them. My boss that hired me, she actually said that I had three kids on probation—she said I have all of those kids' parents on probation.
>
> So it's just, I think that recidivism it just . . . and that revolving door of criminal activity, abuse, neglect, substance abuse. I mean, not even big criminal activity—it's DUIs or marijuana. It's just that aspect, that lifestyle, being socially acceptable.
>
> [PC51/081215]

A prayer person and Sault Tribe member points out the divisive effect that virtual communication, specifically use of cellular devices (texting), internet and social media, may have on healthy family dynamics:

> There are things that we can do to help prevent [suicide] and that comes from turning your computer off and getting back together. It's like when I was a kid, I lived with my mother but I had ten more moms on my street. Every mother that was on that block, you know, they would watch out for each other's children. I don't see that today. I don't see people watching out for the neighbors' kids. And that's sad. That's a . . . that's a social problem again. People just don't care about each other anymore. They're not trying to help each other.
> [PC10/072415]

Field observations support this statement. It is common to view entire families seated for dinner or lunch, with both adults and each child clutching one or even two electronic devices—effectively replacing physical, personal interaction with virtual interaction.

Adolescent and pre-adolescent children have many opportunities to take part in healthy, culturally based activities in the Upper Peninsula area. The Youth Education and Activities program, for instance, provides afterschool and summertime events for middle school–aged children and early teenagers, as well as educational and counseling resources for Ojibwa students attending middle schools in the Seven County Service Area. The Mary Murray Culture Camp on Sugar Island also hosts camps based on spiritual themes, arts and crafts, and traditional seasonal events, such as gathering maple sugar or the "sugar bush" camp. Such educational and cultural experiences, however, may not be readily available to older teenagers and young adults. Coupled with a dearth of job opportunities, interviewees view the lack of physically and mentally healthy activities as a potential source of depression and anxiety for post-adolescent youth.

A cultural program specialist and prayer person also connects the lack of economic opportunity (beyond low-wage part time labor) and opportunities for healthy diversion to the historical "export" of young people from Bowheting; and for those who remain, as incentive to engage in substance use and abuse, and other risky behaviors:

> If we don't find something to engage our young people we're going to lose them. We're either going to lose them to suicide or we're going to lose them to substance abuse. Or we're going to lose them to relocation. It's like I say, our greatest export is our young people. It's a great place to raise kids. It's a safe, nice community. But only until they get to that certain age. Once they hit that certain age, they

> don't qualify for some of these youth programs that they have . . . It's not a whole lot of focus on this at-risk teens, you know, from that age of 13 to 21. That age bracket is . . . survival is tough . . . Again, that's not just a Tribal problem, that's a community problem. It's a social problem.
>
> [PC101/072415]

The words of a Sault Area Schools administrator also express worry over young adults and lack of resources devoted to post-adolescent youth:

> The problem that I see is from 18 to 22 [when] there's no support [for those at risk]. So those students who go from high school to community college or wherever . . . or university, or right to the job field, and they don't have a plan for the rest of their life. Or their plan changes. I'm going to go to Western [Michigan University] and now Western doesn't work for me and now I'm back in the Sault. But Lake State [University] isn't really my dream. There seems to be this feeling of failure. This feeling of I don't know what I want to do. And the supports aren't there, the way that we just throw support at kids K-12, and especially [grades] 6–12. Does that mean that we don't have a problem in this building? Yeah, anytime there's a student who is thinking of harming themselves in any way, or harming another person in any way, that's a problem. We have a lot more resources in place because we have kids every day, 800 at a time that are here. Students have become much better at reporting [self-harm, thoughts of self-harm]. It's a known issue, it's a national issue, and so students are not afraid to walk up to a teacher, a counselor, a parent . . . myself, Mrs. [XXXX], Mrs. [XXXX] and say, this person reported this last night. I'll take it one step further. We've called other districts, other districts have called here, I just had a student report that is friends with one of your kids, they were on Twitter last night reporting they're going to hurt themselves. And so we can follow up on that. The youth that I see the most at risk are that 18 to 22, 23-year-old range. And I don't know if it builds up while they are in high school and they go out and there isn't as much support or if it stems from not being as successful as they hoped to be when they move on. But those are still our kids. And so it hurts.
>
> [PC1/072415]

Unemployment and poverty present distinct challenges for Tribal and non-Tribal families seeking care in the Eastern Upper Peninsula. In 2015, the seven counties in the Sault Tribe's Service Area experienced higher poverty rates (14.6 percent, Alger County—19.7 percent, Chippewa County) and lower median household income ($34,118, Schoolcraft

County—$45,409, Marquette County) than the national averages (13.5 percent and $56,516, respectively) (U.S. Census Bureau, 2015). Residents often respond to lack of jobs and low wages by seeking more than one part-time or full-time position to make ends meet. Community members often point out prevalence of part-time positions as the result of local hiring practices. Business owners, in order to avoid providing health insurance, retirement, vacation time, maternity leave, and other benefits, may hire part-time employees who do not qualify for such benefits. The Sault Tribe enterprises, especially casino operations, reportedly utilize this practice as well.

The hectic nature of working one or two jobs, exacerbated by the demands of tourism and the gambling industry that often requires weekend and late night shifts, may contribute to parents' inability to schedule and attend mental health services for their children, or themselves. In the words of a Sault Area Schools administrator discussing the barriers to mental health care for youth:

> [Y]ou have people with busy schedules, single families with split shifts. They're not all the traditional blue collar or middle class . . . they lack the resources to access appropriate mental health services. [PC11/072215]

"Is he gonna make it?" It was almost 9 a.m. We should've been in the lodge by now. It's important to get a sweat started early in the day, but for different reasons, depending on the season. In the winter, you want to get a sweat lodge started to get in the warm confines of the lodge and escape the cold. In the summer, though, you want to start the sweat as early in the morning as possible in order to avoid the double effect of a sweat lodge and the added heat and humidity of the day.

"I don't know. I think he said he was working last night or it might be that he's working now," said Les. "His schedule is kinda hectic and sometimes when they give him overtime he's gotta take advantage of it." Les walks to the edge of the clearing where the lodge and fire take up the center and plucks a small stick, still green with oak leaves stemming from its body, and returns to his chair. Beckoning me over, he leans forward to draw into the dark brown earth in front of his bare feet. "Have you ever heard of the stages of life?"

"No, I don't think so."

"There are seven points in the path of life," he says, as he continues drawing a serpentine line in the dirt with the fat end of the stick. "Each point represents a change that takes place in our life. With each change comes a new stage, and new responsibilities." He points to the base of the line. "In the first point, we are born. We have a period of innocence as children when we discover our personal direction in life and build foundations of character. Children at that age are not really responsible for what they do. Elders and children of this age spend a lot of time together, teaching and relying on one another. That age," he says, tapping on the first bend in the line, "ends at about 12 or 13 years old, at the second point. This time is our adolescence, where we grow into adulthood."

He continues in this way—

The third point comes at about 18 years old and ends in our mid-20s, when we become young adults and are responsible for providing for the family and the community.

The fourth point is our true adulthood, when we are responsible for raising and providing for a family, while taking on more leadership in the community as we near middle age.

The fifth point happens in our 50s or early 60s, we start to transition into elders—junior elders—leaders in the community who learn to teach as elders.

The sixth point is our elder stage. We teach young ones, and young adults, providing guidance and carrying over our stories and culture.

The final, seventh point of life, comes in the time before we walk on. This is a very important moment, because we have to show courage and ease those we leave behind. Many people, from fear of death, abandon their teachings at this point. But this is a moment to show an example of walking on with composure.

At each stage, an individual is responsible for the wellbeing of one or more generations at different stages within the community. Children learn from elders, and in return the elders are helped by children in their old age. Young adults work alongside older adults. Sons and daughters assist in the heavy labor. In turn those young adults are taught family and community leadership.

Breaking my attention from the figure before us, I tell him, "It's funny. The twig or sapling you're using has seven points, or twists."

He takes the stick in his hand and reviews it. He hands it to me with directions to "pluck away the little stems and leaves. Peel off the bark. You should keep it for a pipe tamper."

Just then, a young man with long black hair in a ponytail, bouncing on the back of a red scooter, pulls into the church parking lot off Marquette Avenue. The obnoxious engine breaks the silence of the clear blue morning as he steers his scooter at a near-idle to the back corner of the parking lot. After turning off the engine and flipping the kick stand down, he plucks a red backpack off the back of the rear rack and jauntily makes his way over to us through the short, beaten path between the brick walled church and two small sheds.

"Boozhoo," he says.

We return the greeting and I add, "Glad you could make it."

"Me too. I really need a good sweat. It's been too long. They got me on some weird schedule lately, so I haven't been able to go as much."

"Still up at the casino?"

"Yep."

He plunks down on one of the weather-beaten stumps to the side of the lodge door, away from the enormous heat of the fire. Several Grandfathers (stones) peak through the burning wood, which, placed in the center of the lodge and doused with cedar water, will create a purifying steam.

"Man, you got that fire going hot, huh?"

"Yeah, I think we're in for it today," I reply.

Absence of mental health services and resources is a common issue in American Indian communities attempting to prevent suicide (Walls, Hautala, and Hurley, 2014; Doll and Brady, 2013). Despite a more robust health care system and the greater availability of master's level counselors in the Sault Tribe, relative to other American Indian reservation communities, interviewees commonly cite the need for resources and services to treat behavioral issues, substance abuse, and suicide ideation. Community members identify a gap in child-psychiatrists as a serious barrier to effective treatment. Questioned about "barriers to mental health assistance," an Anishnaabek Child and Family Services case worker strongly replies:

> No psychiatrists up at the tribe. No psychiatrist. [Which is] huge, huge, huge . . . You got clinicians signing off on other clinicians because they've got their credentials. But we need somebody. We need a . . . that pyramid needs a peak. You know what I'm saying? And when we do get somebody it becomes a golden pen, and really the therapeutic value is really diluted because it becomes a golden pen . . . You get the clinical social workers, nurse practitioners, [and] other people that are doing the assessments. The psychiatrist sees them and then they sign off, where they don't really get the opportunity or the real life [experience] to sit down and have good sessions with them. And even when we have the video conf[erence], the psychiatrist we contact with teleconference, you can only fit so many people in a 40 hour schedule, you know? And we seem to have an inordinate amount of issues here in Sault tribe. I think. I don't know how to compare it with anything else . . . but I do think we have an inordinate amount of issues here. Because we have a lack of resources, at the top where we need them. We do a really good job up at IHS [Indian Health Services], and they do a really good job of getting people in for medical services. There's the nurse practitioners, clinicians . . . but we need that psychiatrist, hands-down. That's the problem, that's the biggest problem I see. The biggest barrier.
>
> [PC12/080515]

A former Sault Area Schools counselor, who is also a licensed social worker, further highlights the unavailability of child psychiatrists, while pointing out potential deficiencies of interactive counseling and evaluations currently used in the Eastern Upper Peninsula:

> [T]his is really a rural area. We're at a huge disadvantage for accessing services for youth when it comes to child psychiatrists and child psychologists. HBH, Hiawatha Behavioral Health, would be our

community mental health here in the community. You have to be [in] pretty severe [condition] to be able to access services there . . . So families then are limited as far as their options. If you have a decent income, you might need to seek out a private practice, and there's some in the community. And you would have [to have] insurance then that would pay for that. Those are usually master level or some psychologists. I can't think of anyone who specializes in and really is a child psychiatrist or child psychologist in this community.

Hiawatha Behavioral Health, in order to access that [psychiatric services] they do . . . like Med TV. It's like interactive TV where they contract with somebody who really very rarely is here on site and is all interactive TV. Like Skype. If you're not seeing a child who may be struggling, is either depressed or bipolar and you're really relying on somebody else's case notes or some of this interactive component . . . that's a huge disadvantage.

When families need to seek those services where they're really on-site, they end up having to travel over to Marquette. That's gonna be a three-hour drive, to really have a very comprehensive evaluation done of their child by a psychiatrist.

[PC11/072215]

Absence of oversight by psychiatrists, or at least pediatricians or medical doctors with specialized training and experience in child psychiatry or psychology, may lead to less informed treatment plans. Existing health care options, however, are beset with nuances of patient–provider interaction, in-take policies, and treatment approaches that may create a sense of distrust between provider and patient.

In order to receive inpatient services at Hiawatha Behavioral Health, for example, a Tribal or non-Tribal person must present a "severe" mental condition. Hiawatha Behavioral Health, however, aware of lower-level counseling services (non-psychiatric, outpatient) at the Sault Tribe Behavioral Clinic, may redirect Sault Tribe members presenting with severe mental health issues to Sault Tribe Indian Health Services—rather than provide Sault Tribe members with inpatient services. Responding to the question of whether or not non-Tribal mental health organizations have a good working relationship with Tribal members, a Sault Tribe Behavioral Health administrator states:

I think there's people at HBH that feel—meaning our coordinating agency in this area—that feel . . . that the tribe is here for a reason and that our patients should come here for care rather than go there. I think they've actually made some of our patients feel that way.

[In] our Tribal community we have the service available to members that most people do not have . . . which is very good, I think . . . But

> HBH feels that a lot of our members, like for psychiatric or even for . . . like when we had a psychiatrist on board they would send all those patients, if they were Tribal members to us to be seen here instead of them taking care of them [at HBH, which] they had an agreement, a legal obligation to do. But that's what they would do . . . they would toss out patients back to us . . . It was bad. I think that when it comes down to admitting some of our tribal members [in a facility], too, like for severe mental impairment, in a situation where they need to be, maybe, held against their will, hospitalized, to get back on their feet again . . . I think that even impacts some of those decisions. They're less likely to get placed . . . as a residential inpatient. So I really think that impacts tribal members at some point in our community.
>
> [PC13/072115]

A family medical doctor and longtime resident of the Eastern Upper Peninsula area provides further insight on potential distrust, as well as how he has built trust, between patient and provider:

> What would prevent them from seeking help? I guess if they've been burned before. Or if they have not had a relationship that's enabled them to trust. I think anyone can think of a person who's had a damaging childhood where they have trust issues. Unfortunately, that is the norm for a lot of people. And those particular people who have trust issues might be the people we can't build a rapport with, they can't open up. They can't share what's going on in their deepest darkest closet. So I can see that happening.
>
> If there is something acutely happening . . . [the] regular doctor office relationships don't work so well with an acute emergent mental issue. Oftentimes if someone calls our office and there is an acute issue, whether it's an acute psychological break, or if they're actively contemplating suicide, staff, rightly so, directs them to emergency services. You need to go to the emergency room. Because then that would be the safest place for them.
>
> Now with that being said, even though it is the safest place, that itself can create a huge barrier. Because here you have the person who is comfortable with the family doctor, who's taken care of them for ten plus years . . . now they're being told that they need to go somewhere else and talk to a stranger about what they're feeling. Even though from a safety aspect it's the best thing, they can't necessarily get the care that they need. So they go into emergency services, they go into the ER. The ER doctor comes in, [asks] what can I do for you today? [Then] they realize they're having suicidal thoughts. Well, the next thing the phone call is to the crisis worker from Hiawatha Behavioral Health. [The] crisis worker shows up after 45 minutes,

> an hour, [the patient] sits and talks with who might be a complete stranger. And talks with him about what's going on and through this whole process again they're not . . . there not getting that rapport with the doctor, they're not getting that feeling that somebody actually cares. I guess it would be akin to, 'oh, you have high blood pressure, this is what you need for high blood pressure.' When in fact what they need is somebody who cares and they feel that that person cares. I know it's an essay question, you're not going to tell me whether I'm right or wrong, but that's what I see is a huge barrier in this community. Yes we have rapport with our patients. Yes we can handle stuff when they walk in and you know they're dealing with stuff we can work on that, but in an emergency situation, that whole system kind of falls apart and they're thrown to this other doctor who cannot give them the same love . . . that their regular doctor can. [PC3/071615]

Lack of on-site psychiatric monitoring, viewed as necessary for safe and effective alteration of medication type and dosage, is being replaced by virtual counseling and off-site supervision. The result of off-site supervision and reliance on virtual, as opposed to direct, monitoring, is described by a Sault Tribe Behavioral Health Center administrator as she relates a case of improper medication:

> I've worked in schools, school settings [for a number of years] . . . and thinking about one [child] in particular who was in the [xxx] grade at a local school. [The child] had a lot of behavioral issues. The family life, though, was pretty chaotic and disruptive, which I'm sure exacerbated whatever was going on with [the child]. But [the child] was a client with Hiawatha Behavioral Health and was on, just . . . probably about eight or nine medications. And one of the severe side effects of one of the medications is that it would cause [symptom]. And this [child] had [the symptom] and the deal was if they developed the [symptom] and you didn't get them off the medicine fairly quickly, then they would have that [symptom] for the rest of their lives, whether you removed them from the medication or not. And other children were starting to tease [the child] because of the [symptom] And so, I worked with the mother and we asked that [the child] be taken off that medication and fortunately [the child] was taken off of it in time that the [symptoms] were not permanent. But I just always thought about that too. If I hadn't been working with the mother, that [child] could've been permanently scarred from that medication that was supposed to help [the child]. And really, even after [the child] was taken off the medication, [the child's] behavior was still pretty good, [the child]

just didn't have that stigma that other children would pick on, you know?

So, yeah, I do think that sometimes people are overly medicated. And I know just from even my own experiences too, children are put on medications because they're disruptive in the classroom. And it's more for the teacher than it is for the child. And sometimes it turns kids into little, kind of zombies almost, you know. They're just not functioning well enough. And of course I've seen it on the flipside too, where the child is struggling a lot academically and then they do get the correct medication and the correct level of medication, and then they really do a lot better, and feel better about themselves. So, I've seen it both ways. But I, really I've seen more of what I consider overmedication than what I consider being a correct amount and a helpful amount. And I don't know why that is.

I just think that maybe, I know there's a shortage of psychiatrists, and a lot of times their only seeing them on ITV, interactive TV. They're not face to face with them. So they get a very small amount of time with them and [can't] do follow-ups. You know, maybe [they follow up] three months down the road. And, you know, with children too, the medications need to be checked on a regular basis because these are growing bodies and growing brains. And so there should be ongoing monitoring, and adjusting to take into account what that person now needs. In my opinion, that doesn't happen well enough.

[PC7/111715]

The community commonly cites an imbalance between treating children with behavioral medications and holistic treatment forms that do not rely, primarily, on medication. According to the above story, and several other interview participants, "drugs, drugs, drugs" have become the relied upon method for treating behavioral and mental issues, as well as stress, anxiety, and emotional pain from traumatic events. This over-reliance on prescription drugs is not a new phenomenon restricted to the Sault Tribe, but rather, is a national issue.

In his in-depth study of the prescription drug industry, *Drugs for Life: How Pharmaceutical Companies Define Our Health*, Joseph Dumit (2012) uncovers the enormous shadow cast by drug companies on the national health care system. For decades, large corporations such as Pfizer used aggressive marketing strategies to persuade Americans that prescription drugs developed along the lines of "evidence based" research are necessary for our physical and mental health. An over-reliance on chemical medication, however, presents a clear danger for children and their developing minds, when the necessary "face to face" monitoring and care is not available. While the above statements describe a system that fails to provide psychiatric care for youth, mental health care, according to the following exchange, as a public health challenge forces providers to react, rather than use creative proactive approaches to mental health care:

SA: How has the mental health community responded to youth suicide?

PUBLIC HEALTH ADMINISTRATOR: Again, I think, when a youth suicide occurs, everybody rallies. I don't know if they're doing anything above and beyond or on a continual basis to address things . . . unless something happens. I mean mental health is a funny . . . [working in] mental health, in general, you work from crisis to crisis. And when you're in mental health, whether that be community mental health or tribal mental health, you have to deal with the here and now, with whatever's happening with that client or whoever walks in the door. And granted you deal with a lot of suicide. A lot of suicide attempts, suicide ideation, all of that . . . But I'm just thinking when I worked in community mental health, I dealt with it and then I had to move on to the next, and I had to move on to the next. So you kind of feel like you are dealing with it all the time. I don't know if you feel like you are ever getting ahead of the curve, though.

SA: It sounds . . . And I don't want to put words in your mouth, it sounds as if you're describing a triage situation . . . would it be safe to say that?

PUBLIC HEALTH ADMINISTRATOR: Yes, it would. [PC8/072015]

The Sault Tribe considers the stigmatization of Tribal members seeking help a serious barrier for those seeking help, as sentiment echoed within American Indian communities nationwide (Grandbois, 2005; Freedenthal and Stiffman, 2007). Stigma, as defined early on in studies by sociologist Irving Goffman, is 'the situation of the individual who is disqualified from full social acceptance' due to a visible or potentially visible characteristic. The fear of being seen as 'different' or 'abnormal' in the eyes of friends, family, or the community may cause those who need mental health care to downplay their problems or not seek help altogether, as described by a local Traditional Healer:

> I think [youth do not seek out help] just out of fear. They don't want to be any more different than they are. You know, we've all been young. We all wanted to fit in. And I think that fear of . . . I know my son was always fearful that someone would find out he was on medication, you know, and what he was being treated for. And he didn't want anyone to know. You know, it was just his close personal family I guess that kinda knew. So, in most cases I think it's just fear or even, again, it comes down to the families not wanting to admit

that there's more going on than just the different things that their son, daughter might have going on with them. That there might be some real psychological issues going on.

[PC9/080515]

Family may perpetuate an individual fear of stigma as well. As stated by a Sault Area Schools counselor, a person's "upbringing and belief system may be" one that suppresses an expression of mental health problems, or issues that may reflect poorly on the family:

> You don't air your dirty laundry, you don't seek services. You keep it within your household, your family and you deal with it yourself. So I think sometimes it might be part of your generation, it might be part of your educational background or experience that affects a family's willingness to seek out counseling services, that it is an appropriate thing to do as a parent and not a sign of weakness.
>
> [PC5/081215]

The counselor continues to describe concern over the role of parents in a child's attempt to seek help:

> In the past it's [not seeking mental health treatment or counseling has] been because they're gonna get made fun of, the stigma of going to counseling. And a lot of it, aside from that, is their parents won't allow it. Believe it or not I've had parents who won't allow it. 'There's nothing wrong with my kid, they don't need to go.'
>
> When youth in the past have said that they're going to counseling, you know, their friends will be like, 'what do you mean? are you crazy?' You know, they get that, 'you're so messed up you need to go to counseling.' And 'you're crazy . . . do you have multiple personalities?' I've heard that one thrown out because you're going to counseling, 'do you hear voices?' So there's all that stigma going there, that it's shameful to ask for help. That you should be able to do it yourself. Especially if their friends don't have those issues, what do you mean you have to go talk to somebody?
>
> . . . if it's an issue with their parents, they don't want their parents to know what they're doing, what they're feeling. Or if they have an issue with the parent, you know, if they're being abused by the parent, they don't want their parents to know that they're going to go to counseling and to talk about verbal abuse or even if they're being beat. Because then they bring in the parent, they don't want to talk [and] they shut down. They're not accomplishing anything and then the counselors always going to take the parents' side. Those are the issues that we face.

In other instances, the school counselor was informed that students can "see me [the counselor], but they can't see a mental health provider," a statement that may stem from a sense of distrust of mental health providers, fear of stigma, or a combination of these or other factors. A Sault Area Schools administrator also describes the impact that fear of stigma can have on the effectiveness of suicide prevention efforts, specifically when schools provide students with counseling services in response to traumatic events:

> Mental health assistance is definitely there. There's a stigma that goes along with that, and I will have a lot of students tell me that mental health doesn't help them, doesn't help them. They are also not super open to overcoming the stigma, to try and reach out for help.
>
> [PC10I1/072415]

A social dynamic existing at Tribal health centers themselves may create anxiety for individuals attempting to access services, stemming from a fear of "rumor" and being "found out" by family and community members. In response to the question of whether or not patients have brought up concerns over confidentiality or the possibility that the community could learn of medical or mental health care related visits, a medical provider at Sault Tribe Health Center states:

> Sure, that's always a concern. I mean, so at a tribal clinic like . . . like the Sault Tribal health center is . . . it is . . . our patients are tribal members, but our staff is also [composed of] tribal members. So the issue of confidentiality with both mental health as well as physical health issues is always one of real importance. And there are definitely tribal members that don't come to our clinics because they feel like their family or their neighbors or whatever, that are working there, and they're just going to know everything about them. And, so that crosses the line with mental health. Then . . . and of course we are HIPAA [bound by Hippocratic oath to maintain patient-provider confidentiality] compliant. And we have electronic health records and we can track, you know, when people breach that, breach those electronic health records and breach confidentiality. So, it's . . . probably even more stringently [supervised] than in other places. But there's definitely that kind of feeling in the, in some members of the tribe, I know not all, but in some.
>
> [PC4/082115]

Many Tribal members also pursue traditional medicine, which represents a holistic view of health and wellness that addresses personal lifestyle, family and home settings, use of natural medicines (along or in safe combination with Western medicine), one's sense of identity and purpose and spirituality. Due to the informal nature of traditional medicine clinics and the cultural acceptability of traditional medicine, seeking traditional medicine does not transfer stigma upon the patient. Traditional healers employed by the Sault Tribe health center, however, are often unavailable due to strenuous workloads and wide geographical area of responsibility requiring constant travel.

At the same time, a sense of conflicted identity may lead to a hesitation for Tribal members in approaching traditional healers and traditional-spiritual activities (sweat lodges, Wabano lodge, and so on). A lack of previous experience with "Indian ways" and a resulting strangeness towards traditional activities (I have never participated in that before/I did not grow up with that), some Tribal members may avoid or be reluctant to participate in what could be very helpful healing ceremonies.

Works Cited

Cleland, C. E. (1992) *Rights of Conquest: The History and Culture of Michigan's Native Americans*. Ann Arbor: University of Michigan Press.

Doll, J., and Brady, K. (2013) "Project HOPE: Implementing Sensory Experiences for Suicide Prevention in a Native American Community." *Occupational Therapy in Mental Health*. 29 (2), 149–158.

Dumit, J. (2012) *Drugs for Life: How Pharmaceutical Companies Define Our Health*. Durham, NC: Duke University Press.

Freedenthal, S., and Stiffman, A. (2007) "'They Might Think I Was Crazy': Young American Indians' Reasons for Not Seeking Help When Suicidal." *Journal of Adolescent Research*. 22 (1), 58–77.

Grandbois, D. (2005) "Stigma of Mental Illness Among American Indian and Alaska Native Nations: Historical and Contemporary Perspectives." *Issues in Mental Health Nursing*. 26 (10), 1001–1024.

Herne, M., Bartholomew, M., and Weahkee, R. (2014) "Suicide Mortality Among American Indians and Alaska Natives, 1999–2009." *American Journal of Public Health*. 104 (Suppl 3), S336–S342.

Herring, R. (1994) "Substance Use Among Native American Indian Youth: A Selected Review of Causality." *Journal of Counseling and Development*. 72 (6), 578–584.

Olson, L., and Wahab, S. (2006) "American Indians and Suicide: A Neglected Area of Research." *Trauma, Violence & Abuse*. 7 (1), 19–33.

Overmier, B. and Seligman, M. (1967) "Effects of Inescapable Shock Upon Subsequent Escape and Avoidance." *Journal of Comparative and Physiological Psychology*. 63 (1), 28–33.

"Quickfacts, Income and Poverty" by County. Accessed February 22, 2017. www.census.gov/quickfacts/table/AFN120212/26033

RAPID Assessment for Adolescent Preventive Services Survey Data (generated 2009–2015 at Sault Area High School) Courtesy of Chippewa County Health Department.

Sault Tribe, Grant Application. "Sault Tribe Alive Youth (STAY) Project 2008." Grant #1U79SM058400-01. OIA. Accessed August 10, 2014.

Seligman, M. (1972) "Learned Helplessness." *Annual Review of Medicine*. 23 (1), 407–412.

"U.S. Census Bureau, Income and Poverty in the United States: 2015." Accessed February 22, 2017. www.census.gov/library/publications/2016/demo/p60-256.html

Walls, M., Hautala, D., and Hurley, J. (2014) "'Rebuilding Our Community': Hearing Silenced Voices on Aboriginal Youth Suicide." *Transcultural Psychiatry*. 51 (1), 47–72.

SA: *What is suicide?*

SCHOOL COUNSELOR: *Suicide is an individual's attempt to try and stop pain, without really knowing that they are causing great pain to another. It's a selfish act.*

SA: *Are there good reasons for suicide or reasons that are socially acceptable?*

SCHOOL COUNSELOR: *No. Point blank, no.*

SA: *In other interviews, some people have said very similar [answers], you know, have said that and then described . . . well . . . let's say someone is older or is in great pain or something along those lines . . . they said that they may or may not still accept it, but that they can understand it and the community may understand it as well. What are your thoughts on that?*

SCHOOL COUNSELOR: *Like specifically the young lady who had cancer of the brain. Cancer that, what was it, last year? She did the medically induced . . . I don't know, I guess I just think all life is precious. And I can understand why she did what she did, like that case specifically, and I know that there have been others. I guess if the quality of life is what's in question, there might be circumstances. I don't know that I could personally say for myself that that would ever come in, you know? That's because I think, like I said, because all life is precious. So I guess I really, I don't know. Having never had anybody in my life that's been that bad. Do I think what she did was wrong? No. I think for her, she felt that that was the right thing and I guess it does come down to personal choice for those circumstances. But a 16-year-old kid who's healthy? No. It's just an emotional crisis, that's stuff that can be helped.*

SA: *Um hmm. In the community, in the Sault tribe community, is suicide seen as an acceptable death or an unacceptable death?*

SCHOOL COUNSELOR: *I would hope unacceptable. I mean I'm not a . . . I wasn't raised culturally, so I can't speak from the cultural aspect. There's stuff that I learned myself as an adult. Because my mom grew up in a time period where it was shameful to be native.*

SA: *Um hmm.*

SCHOOL COUNSELOR: *So I wasn't raised culturally. But I don't know exactly how one of our elders would view that from a cultural aspect. But . . . I kind of lost my train of thought (laughs).*

SA: *Well, the question was, in the community eyes, is suicide seen as acceptable or unacceptable?*

SCHOOL COUNSELOR: *No. I would hope not.*

SA: *Do you feel that the youth that you've interacted with, do you feel like they find it to be acceptable or unacceptable?*

SCHOOL COUNSELOR: *The youth that I've worked with, I would say, think it's unacceptable. Even the youth that are contemplating it. But they've reached a point where they think they have no other option . . . And those are the cases that break your heart, because nobody should ever be made to feel that their life is not important.* [PC5/081215]

SENATOR TESTER: *. . . Senator Udall went down to the litany of things that you're facing in Indian Country in his opening statement. Alcohol, drug abuse, physical abuse, poor nutrition, poor schools, domestic violence, poverty, overcrowded housing. And, you know the statistics probably better than anybody up here . . . Native Americans commit suicide the highest of any minority in the country [amongst] 15–34 year olds, [at] twice the rate of anybody else.*

What do we do about this? I mean, if I'm dealing, and personally if myself or my kids, if there's alcohol abuse, drug abuse by parents or the potential person who is going to commit suicide, combine that with poor nutrition, poor schools, where do you start?

DR. LAFROMBOISE: *Well, first of all, I understand what you're alluding to. You're alluding to all these intense social determinants of behavior.*

SENATOR TESTER: *Bingo.*

DR. LAFROMBOISE: *And probably, you're thinking I'm naive to focus on the individual.*

SENATOR TESTER: *No, no. I want to know what to do to solve the problem.*

DR. LAFROMBOISE: *Okay. Here's what I would suggest, okay, to all these problems that need to be solved. But one thing that we do know about the resilience literature is that the children who are resilient are able—who are—that means they are able to thrive in spite of all this adversity, are children who are able to manage their emotions and/or able to stay detached from situations and they are able to have a strong identity and all these things, that these kinds of, these programs do. They are emphasizing the protective factors.*

SENATOR TESTER: *So the resilience is taught where? In school?*

DR. LAFROMBOISE: *It can start—resilience begins as a child. Children learn this when they cry . . .*

SENATOR TESTER: *I know. But when you've got dysfunction and alcoholism and housing problems, where the hell are they going to learn the resilience?*

June 25, 2015 Senate Committee on Native American Affairs Hearing: "Demanding Results to End Native Youth Suicides."

5 Prevention

An Approach to Mental Health Care and Treatment Models, and Indicator of Social and Cultural Values

To me, suicide prevention is . . . properly educating our people—especially our young people—about . . . or recognizing when our young people are in those areas of whether it's being bullied or just [when] their life might be a little bit hard, to recognize the signs sooner than we have been in the past. And getting some kind of help for the people, whether young or old. And I think it's about recognizing those patterns and those signs of when people are going towards the suicide and suicide thoughts and taking them seriously, even if some might say, 'oh, that person always says that.' Even in my family we've had that . . . and we thought that person never would do it and they have. So I think, to me, [prevention] is about us being proactive and doing our best to do whatever we can to help our people that might be in a situation of being suicidal as much as we can.

—Sault Tribe Traditional Medicine Healer [PC93/102715]

[Prevention is] making sure that people have the resources to work out their problems. An example would be for employees. We have an employee assistance program, so with new employee orientation we make it very clear that if you ever have any issue you feel you need to talk about the employee assistance program's available. So I think that would be a resource available to employees. As well as for tribal members with the health centers, behavior health department. But also not only that type of setting, but the spiritual setting as well. Spiritual leaders, drum keepers and stuff like that. I think those types of resources.

—Sault Tribe Member and Cultural Program Specialist [PC6/080615]

The literature on youth suicide is replete with discussion and investigation of risk factors, resilience, protective factors, areas of community strength, and similar terminology. The goal of studying the development and relationships between risk and protective factors present in communities' experiences of youth suicide (i.e., relationship between substance abuse and self-harm, buffer effects of risk and protective factors) revolves around effective prevention. Yet, the literature displays little effort at answering or even forming the question—a question that circled back on itself repeatedly during the fieldwork portions of this work, which is, *What is suicide prevention*? For interviewees, many of whom are responsible for formulating or facilitating prevention measures, suicide prevention includes:

- Educating on the topic of suicide in multiple venues and audiences—children in schools; adults, specifically adults who work with youth, (i.e., child welfare agencies, schools, mental health programs, and extracurricular programs)
- Providing counseling to individuals contemplating, actively planning, attempting suicide
- Promoting healthy activities and pleasant settings (i.e., parks, facilities, afterschool programs, culturally based programs) to provide alternatives to risk behaviors, as well as instill a sense of belonging, purpose, and community
- Teaching coping mechanisms and concept of resilience directly to youth (how to respond to anger, depression, uncontrollable forces)
- Enhancing the availability and scope of mental health services
- Advertising emergency support, having emergency support on hand throughout the community (i.e., suicide hotlines, mental health evaluators in emergency rooms)
- Addressing substance abuse and other common contributing factors through education and intervention

If we were to 'get semantic,' however, about the concept of prevention, we can redefine many responses summarized above as 'interventative.' For instance, stopping an individual from completing suicide is an 'intervention,' with the person responding to a suicide attempt intervening or getting between attempt and completion; or between suicide ideation and plan to complete suicide, and an attempt to fulfill that plan. Going further, providing mental health care may help an individual suffering from suicidal ideation or risk factors (e.g., depression, hopelessness); however, an awareness of mental health resources and encouragement to see a counselor does not 'prevent' the suicidal ideation already occurring. A Sault Area public health professional addresses the apparent contradiction or confusion over prevention and intervention:

> I think people misuse prevention and intervention. True prevention to me is providing education, tools, whatever, before a thought has even entered anyone's mind of suicide . . . True prevention is . . . you're starting to educate about the issue before there's ever even an inkling of the issue. And that's how we manage everything in public health. It's like . . . before you become obese, let me teach you the tools from the time you're three on[ward] how to eat appropriately,

> so that you know what is, so you don't have to intervene when you're fifty pounds overweight. I think a lot of people think prevention is, 'you're suicidal, so I'm going to prevent you from completing your suicide.' That's actually intervention.
>
> [PC8/072015]

"True prevention," in this sense, occurs *before* risk factors can cause harm. Providing resources (e.g., education, supporting life skills, reducing social determinants of health) "before a thought has even entered anyone's mind of suicide," and the definition of intervention as an attempt to assist individuals after they are at risk, is a clear separation from the majority of interviewees' and researchers' conceptualization of prevention and intervention. Providing resources and assistance to an individual before suicide ideation (prevention) or directly intervening after "a thought has even entered anyone's mind," however, outlines the individual as a suicidal object. Simultaneously, a health focus on the individual, however, may divert attention from multi-level factors influencing suicide trends for ethnic groups (Walls, Hautala, and Hurley, 2014).

SA: *Why did youth suicide become a significant issue in the Sault tribe community?*

CULTURAL PROGRAMS ADMINISTRATOR/HELPER: *Why? I don't think that it's just a Sault tribe thing. It's all people have that problem. I think it's kind of a bigger problem for . . . for Indian country. Not just the Sault tribe or just Bay Mills but all of Indian country because of the stigmatisms that are left over. Those blood memories that they have of the boarding school era—just those family histories. Through the boarding school they took away our ability to parent. They would come and take our children, from about the time they were three or four years old and they would keep them until they were eighteen, nineteen. Some of them were lucky enough to get yearly visits for Christmas, but that's it. That's all they got. Other than that they stayed in those homes and they were taught how to be institutional. But that didn't teach them anything of how to raise children, because they were in these mass homes, and they didn't have the ability to deal with stress. They didn't have our own coping mechanisms that we had before that time. We were able to teach our children from the time they were little. And that boarding school time that took our kids away, our parents became lost and started to turn to alcohol. Back in those days the biggest problem that they had was the alcoholism. And as the years progressed, pharmaceuticals started coming into play and all of those other drugs and craziness. And then they take these kids that are eighteen, nineteen years old, they turn them loose on the world thinking they're going to be productive citizens but they don't know how. They didn't have social interactions. It just . . . it wasn't allowed. And that took away from some of our original teachings, [what] some of our original thoughts were about.*

Wiitokaage. I've been told that's the last thing that the creator tells us before we come into this world—Wiitokaage, is help one another. A lot of people had lost that philosophy. You know, just that simple word can mean so much. Wiitokaage, very small when you look at the word but when you define it and you look at the meaning that goes with it and the story, that's all a part of that word. People could actually base their lifestyle just on that one word. And if we had more people that would incorporate that into their daily thinking, we wouldn't have the same kind of problems that we have.

Nowadays, with these . . . the social media and the information explosion, some of our parents, they're sober and clean but now they've found the computers. They've found this time and they're not interacting with their children. So . . . it's a problem that I call the digital disconnect. People are digitally disconnected from their children and from their communities and their families. And that's, I would attribute that to being a big part of what's going on with society, not just Indian people but society itself. The parents, aunties, and uncles have just become so engrossed with social media, looking at Facebook, checking Twitter and all of these things and spend all day [on social media], and never doing anything with their children.

Their children need that time, they need that interaction. They need to be able to go out and play and learn how to be a kid. Learn how to understand the seven grandfather teachings: love, respect, bravery, humility, honesty, wisdom, and truth. All of these things that we base our lives on are being lost to . . . are families that are just disconnected. Families that have been in this area for generations and generations are now being split apart because they think they have that anonymity behind the keyboard. They think they can say whatever they want. Families are being torn apart. Our kids are hurting from it because they don't have that, that social interaction to help them deal with other people, how to be able to deal with just life itself. So that's my thoughts on that (chuckles) . . . [PC101/072415]

Finally, I see Brother John strolling into the pow-wow grounds. Like many, I see him as a great source of knowledge and am excited to talk to him about my research on youth suicide. But I hold back, thinking it would be rude to rush the elder before he has a chance to greet various friends and sit under the shade for a moment. Walking around the circuit again, I see the young man sitting next to him vacating the red lawn chair as he responds to a call over the loudspeakers to come up and sing. Brother John seems relaxed and unoccupied, so I take advantage of the moment. I sit and we talk a bit.

"You'll have to forgive me, I don't have tobacco on me," I say, "but I have a braid of Sweet Grass," which I offer up to him in exchange for his insight on a specific oral history, a prophecy, to be specific. We speak for a short time about oral traditions and history for a moment, when he says, "a lot of our teachings are really more for everyday use . . . everyday conduct. It's down to earth," he said.

"So I am doing research on youth suicide . . . and I think it should be told as kind of a story and I don't . . . I'm not sure how to tell it, because . . . Well, first off, it should be told as a story because that's how our people told things."

"A lot of the way that these things are described are . . . it's very negative," he said. Our people don't talk about those things so negatively. The word suicide is not known to our language. As far as I know, that word doesn't exist. The closest thing is, I believe . . . it's Saaganing a person without love or a person who is not loved. That love comes from the community," he continues. "If there is a community that is out there who loves them, then they will be loved because their spirit will be drawn towards that. But a lot of people don't get that love," he concludes, because they are raised by parents addicted to alcohol or drugs, are in an abusive relationship, or family may not be around at all. He returns to the issue of positivity. "Our people would always talk about things that dealt with health with a positive light. You reduce the negative by speaking about the positive, emphasizing the positive."

We talk for a short time longer. I have learned, however, that it is best not to bombard a person with questions, or to force questions. Rather, conversations and 'teachings' happen when and where they will. Before leaving, I ask Brother John if he needs anything—food, water? He politely declines, and we say Baamaa-pii—See you later—often shorted to Baamaa.

Walking around the circuit, with the smell of frybread lingering in the air, wearing against my temptation to snack, I think about that word—Saaganing—a person without love. If a person who is suicidal is Saaganing, without love, then is a state of death equal to living without love? Can a body walk, talk, and according to an Ojibwa understanding, not be alive? Is the difference between life and death, being alive or not being alive, incumbent on the presence or absence of love, community, and relationships? [FN20/071915]

. . . *Our pimaadiziiwin as Anishnaabek people is when we say Miigwech to the creator for this pimaadiziiwin. And we're not just thanking him for the life that we have, but our pimaadiziiwin is we're actually thanking him for the good life that we know is there. And by following within the teachings of what the pimaadiziiwin is, is adhering to our seven grandfather teachings the best that we can. And our pimaadiziiwin actually . . . it does . . . is actually it does . . . it stems, you know, I mean the kind of roots of what pimaadiziiwin means is that we all live within . . . to always be respectful. Always be truthful. Always have courage, you know, to not only have wisdom but to accept those teachings that will give you the wisdom. And to always be humble and [have] humility, you know. To always be honest and most of all, to love. To love who we are as a person and to love our people. I mean, love all people, you know. It doesn't just say that pimaadiziiwin is just for us to do to with, for our people. No, it's to love all life. Black, white, red, yellow, what have you. And for me, what that means to me is that I help anyone . . . the best I can, if I can. You know, a story for me, the things that I've done is, I mean you can ask my wife, we'd stop on the side of the road to change old people's tires. You know, because they're just kind of older people, they're trying to get it and I'll get out and I'll do it. You know, I mean . . . just doing those little things, I guess, you feel what that pimaadiziiwin is, because you asked nothing for it. You're doing it because of your respect and love for the people. And so that's what I do my best to, you know. I mean, I was standing in line to get some prescription at Walgreens one time, and there was kind of a . . . there was a worker there that took care of some old people somewhere, and the one old person, whoever it was . . . was $14 short on their prescriptions, and he was trying to get the person at Walgreens, to say, I'll go back to get it from this person, but they need this medicine, it's a timed medicine. He was doing everything he could to explain and he personally didn't have the money to get this old person's prescription. And I was the next one in line, I said, I'll cover it. And he looks at me and he says, what? And I said I'll cover it. $14, no problem. This whole person you're talking about needs this medication, right? He goes, well, yeah. And I think he drove it from a town somewhere else or something, because he said he had to drive back and they won't give me the meds. And I said I'll cover* *the $14 so you can go back and give them their medicine. And he looked at me and said, but why would you do that? You don't even know the person. And I said I don't have to know the person, but I know a lot of elders that need their medication. I know that I need my medication that's why I'm here. And let's not question it, just let me pay the $14 so you can be on your way. And I'm not doing it just so you can get out of my way, I'm doing it because it's an elder. And he said, well, thank you. So the person took my 14 bucks and that was done. So it's like, you're continuously giving back what you can, when you can, but at the same time you know, you gotta have boundaries too, you know, so . . . So pimaadiziiwin to me, anyways, is so much. And it's kind of just briefly what I can tell you, but knowing that it is about thanking the creator for this good life that we have. But in conjunction with that is doing your best, the best that you can to live a good life. Yep.* [PC9/102715]

Seen as a matter of how—*how* do we approach suicide as a problem and *how* do we implement prevention as a process—prevention becomes an entry point for understanding social views on treatment, medicine, health, and illness (ideological views; see below). Suicide prevention, viewed as a reaction to sickness or illness, exposes the ethnomedical or medical-cultural framework that implicitly guides our approaches to medicine, individual and community health, treatment, and similar terms as processes and products of medicine. In other words, how a society uses medicine and implements treatment is heavily reliant on *ideas* of treatment—in this case preventative or interventative treatment—and the social power, meanings, values, and symbols attributed to treatment and treatment processes. Suicide prevention is a process that emphasizes the individual as object of treatment and catalyst for treatment (prevention). Responses to "what is suicide prevention?" and "how can we prevent youth from turning to suicide as an option?" bear this out:

> [A]ctivities and resources that people have in order to . . . eliminate suicide or prevent people from killing themselves or attempting to do so . . . availability of mental health and substance abuse services, and easier access to them . . . teaching lay people . . . family members and peers about the signs and symptoms of when people are more likely to attempt suicide, and to look out for some of those warning signs . . . I think it was the state that have, that had programs where they give away free locks for guns, so to try to keep those out of the hands of maybe impulsive or intoxicated young people. And so I think that program has helped. So it's really, I think, multifaceted ways in which we can help others prevent suicide . . .
>
> Sault Tribe Mental Health Administrator [PC7/120715]

> I think suicide prevention is creating awareness of the issue so that we hopefully have, we hopefully create safety nets for youth or for anyone considering suicide to access instead of taking their own lives.
>
> Sault Tribe Medical Professional [PC4/083115]

> From a community perspective there's all the things that are engaged in, you know, identifying, treating early, recognizing . . . treating early and getting effective treatments to deal with the issue both medical and behavioral health and all those things so . . . So at all levels from self to family and friends. And I think that the key area really is self and family and friends. I think that's where . . . We were talking a little bit about the board and what actions they . . . I think they want to say, well, what can you do about suicide, what can your department do about suicide what can this department do about suicide? When in fact I think we need to really be self-evaluating . . . and say

> what can we do both in our families and communities to actually do something about it. I think that's . . . that's really gonna be the approach that's gonna be the most effective suicide prevention, is if you get people recognizing in themselves when their thinking is getting a little crooked, not healthy, and to actually do something about that positively. And have family and friends that recognize something's not healthy and not good. And do something about that.
>
> Sault Tribe Mental Health Administrator [PC13/072115]

> Addressing the whole child and ensuring that they have the coping skills. Once again going back to the coping skills, if there is a dysfunctional issue at home or a substance abuse or something along those lines that disrupts a young person's life, going back to coping skills was an answer.
>
> Sault Area Schools Administrator [PC11/072815]

These interview responses and gray literature from local and national sources (e.g., Reed, 2017; STAY grant #1U79SM058400-01, 2008; Michigan Association for Suicide Prevention, 2012; Michigan Department of Health and Human Services, accessed 2017) expose a prevention model composed of two areas of focus that encircles the at-risk individual. The inner circle provides coping mechanisms, builds resilience, and monitors and makes mental health services available for the individual at risk for suicide. The outer circle includes similar treatment methods, while making the community responsible for combating stigma, educating the community, and recognizing and treating a general, non-descript at-risk person throughout the community and its various social institutions (i.e., schools, businesses, and government) (see Figure 5.1).

Specific treatment methods and practices further exhibit a focus on the 'at-risk individual.' Like many departments within the Sault Tribe, the mental health department often works to promote culturally based and enjoyable activities for youth in order to enhance life skills, instill individual resilience and coping mechanisms, and encourage positive social behavior. Program language commonly, if unwittingly, equates "at-risk" with "Indian" or "Traditions." This association is supported by a Sault Tribal Health Center administrator's description of programming designed for at-risk youth:

> We get a lot of youth in our program. And we also participate with the Warrior camp, which is held every summer. The traditional medicine program hosts that, but we also have practitioners that assist during that camp. And that's for *at-risk adolescent males*. And we also provide funding to pay for the food for that camp for the males.

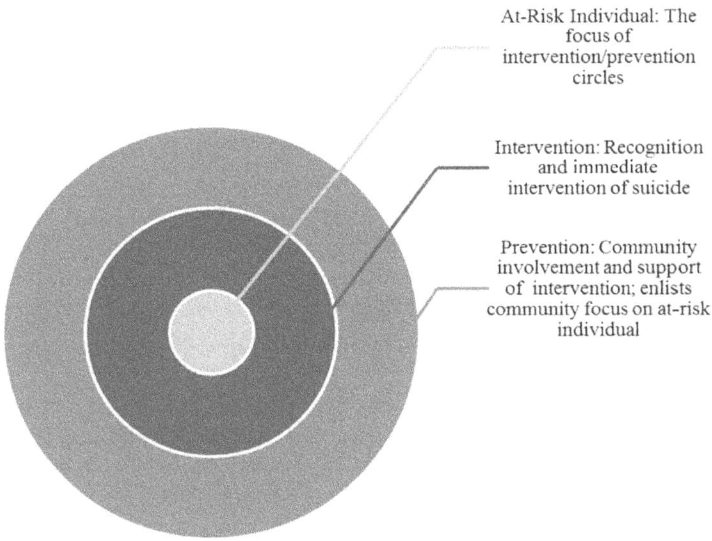

Figure 5.1 Current prevention model

> And we offer a girl's life skills camp every summer that's also a week long, and our staff conducts that. And that's for *at-risk adolescents*. Between both camps we probably had total enrollment of about forty to fifty kids in the summertime. And . . . we have [XXXX], who specializes in play therapy. And we get referrals from a variety of sources for working with the youth. So that's a service that we're very good at. And so we do have quite a bit of access to the young people.
> [PC7/110315]

The primary use of traditional activities (Sugar-Bush camp, Warrior camp, fasting ceremony, sweat lodges, teaching or talking circles) as a response to being "at-risk" is a new phenomenon. Older generations, for instance, do not associate traditional activities with 'at-risk status.' Rather, Ojibwa ceremonies and coming of age events were a matter of course during one's upbringing. Fasting, receiving one's name, and celebrating a child's first hunt ensured that the community continuously recognized and celebrated the youth, eventually accepting the child as a responsible adult. On more than one occasion, elders who have heard of these activities or even helped facilitate activities, such as the Warrior camp, a fasting and teaching camp for young men, joyfully reminisced on their own coming of age ceremonies and experiences.

Such events were not a response to being at risk, but were culturally accepted ways of attaining pimaadziiwin a good life or sense of balance, from an early age. In contrast, current generations are encouraged to take part in Ojibwa ceremonies and activities *in response to* becoming "at risk."

The continued use of language and imagery portraying certain youth as "at-risk" and focusing on the individual also presents in the local high school environment. An (apologetically) long interview excerpt touches on local high school students. Identified as "at-risk" for dropping out of high school, due to academic performance or misbehavior, a minority of students are sent to Malcolm High School, considered by many in the Tribal and non-Tribal community as an alternative school:

SA: Okay. To go back on that again, because this is . . . this is very interesting. Why do you think it is like that, as you said: about 50 percent of the students in the alternative school are native . . . yet, the population at the high school is 30 percent native? So that's a disparity that you could say is significant. So why do you think that disparity exists?

ADMINISTRATOR: I've thought about that a long time. I thought about that a long time. I think some of it is historical in [that] here you have some parents who have graduated from the alternative program when it was in a different location. And they are more comfortable with the idea. We've switched our focus of the alternative program to a credit recovery program. Okay, so it's completely voluntary to go. And so a lot of the students that graduate from the alternative program go there as seniors in high school because they're short two credits, three credits, and it's easier to make it up in the alternative program with the smaller class sizes so they can finish on time.

SA: Um hmm.

ADMINISTRATOR: So the numbers are a bit deceiving in that regard. The bigger identifier is obviously socioeconomic in that population at Malcolm. So I attribute some of it to the socioeconomic aspect. But I really attribute a lot of it to, its smaller class sizes and it's more individualized. And a lot of the students that attend Malcolm don't . . . they're not into playing football. They're not robotics club team members. They like the real individualized one-on-one attention, and they want to get their education, I hate to say done, but finish it up. Know what the plan is, have the supports in place and then move on to the next step. School is not as [all] encompassing with all the extracurricular activities that we offer. They see school as a place that they have to get through, has been my perception. And in the smaller atmosphere, it doesn't hurt that . . . [the Malcolm high school principle] is native, 50, probably more than that, 50 percent. She knows all of the parents, she graduated with a lot of them. Like I said, she's on the tribal board, or on the parent advisory committee. She is super involved and knows a lot of people. In that regard, people have felt more comfortable with the stigma of alternative education. So we view the alternative in this building, we view, I view the alternative education program as part of our programming to make sure every student gets a high school diploma. And for some it means a smaller atmosphere.

SA: One more question on that—

ADMINISTRATOR: Sure.

SA: —and then I'll go on to the questions that are actually written down. So if some students prefer that teaching format, teaching and learning format

ADMINISTRATOR: Um hmm.

SA: yet they're . . . for all intents and purposes they're receiving the same instruction as anyone else, correct?

ADMINISTRATOR: Um hmm.

SA: Why is it called alternative school?

ADMINISTRATOR: I think it's a name that has stuck around for the 40 years that it's been in existence. That the diploma says Malcolm High School . . .

SA: Um hmm.

ADMINISTRATOR: the alternative label comes from some of the programming aspects that are offered and some of the state funding streams, quite honestly. So, I guess that the bigger question that I've heard asked a lot is, why is this the high school and that is Malcolm High School. Societal maybe. It has to be. I tell parents all the time that the diplomas are the same. They don't look any different. And when you [look], the only difference is the signature at the bottom. [The principle of Malcolm] signs a Malcolm High School diploma and [the principle of Sault High] signs the Sault High diploma, and when you ship them off to Michigan Tech or Western, nobody really knows. It is . . . it's an EUP question. It's more of a Sault Sainte Marie question.

SA: So that's . . . so whenever you receive funding for that particular component of the school, the state or whatever funding source actually has within their language the word alternative?

ADMINISTRATOR: There's alternative language in state law. They're also a Title I building, we are not. So there's federal funds involved there as well. But graduation rate information, if you attend an alternative school, is different. The way you report your graduation information to the state is different than it is for a regular high school. And I'm by no means an expert on this. That's one specific example. They offer flex Friday programming, which means if all of your work is complete by Thursday and you have made it through school Monday through Thursday for three weeks in a row or whatever, however they set their calendar up, then Friday is a day to come in and meet with your teacher, and if you're caught up where you need to be, then Friday ends up being a day that you're rewarded and do not have to . . . you can take a long weekend basically. So there, I guess when we say yes, we offer the exact same programming, we offer the exact same classes. They're delivered in other ways and there are different incentive programs that wouldn't work in a population of eight or nine hundred people. At least effectively.

SA: Right, exactly. Are the students who go to the . . . to Malcolm, are they stigmatized by fellow students or anybody else in the community?

ADMINISTRATOR: Yep . . . Yes. And I will say that eight or nine years ago when I started this profession, when I decided to [work at Sault High], [XXXX] was the alternative school principal. And we worked very, very hard—still do—in removing the stigma. At that point you were sent to the alternative building for being a bad student. It was not about education, it was about discipline. If you want to the alternative building you didn't come back. You graduated from Malcolm. There was never a return to Sault High. And a lot of that it's been seven . . . seven years now. So, it takes longer than seven years to remove a stigma. A lot of the stigma with Malcolm High School versus Sault High is honestly parent driven. They [say], 'I don't want my kid going down there. I don't want my kid to attend Malcolm, I want them to graduate from Sault High.' It is, it is seen as a lesser education and I don't believe it is. The assistant principal [XXXX], who hired in last year, came as the math teacher from Malcolm. All of the students start out of this building and for various reasons by the time they're sophomores or juniors in high school the population transfers there. And we work very hard to get rid of that stigma because students probably see the stigma less than their parents do. And so they will fight with their parents to try and attend Malcolm for the reasons that they see that they need in their own education. And sometimes that can go as far as, 'I'm purposely going to fail classes until there's no other option.' The problem with that is the longer you fail classes, the longer it takes you to graduate. So it's not the correct answer to an issue that is perceived. [PC1/072415]

In the case of Malcolm High School, the moniker of "alternative" becomes almost synonymous with "at-risk," leading to parents' disapproval of children attending ("I don't want my kid going down there"). This perception was perpetuated by previous administrators' use of Malcolm as a tool for disciplining or 'getting rid of' disruptive students ("[in the past Malcolm] was not about education, it was about discipline"). While current administrators treat Malcolm as a student resource, promoting different teaching methods, educational schedules, and classroom environments for those experiencing difficulty in traditional learning environments, the earlier stigma of being an "alternative school" student is still present in the Tribal and non-Tribal community.

The feeling that Malcolm successfully provides a comfortable academic environment is echoed by half a dozen young men (Sault Tribe members), who spoke about their experiences at both Sault High and Malcolm. The students who were sent to Malcolm not only preferred Malcolm, but said if faced with returning to Sault High, they would purposefully disrupt their own academic progress or misbehave until they were sent back. One student stated (jokingly) that he would hit a teacher to "get transferred back" to Malcolm, where more one-on-one interaction and support can be had. Malcolm students simply perform at higher levels when exposed to a more personalized teaching style and learning environment.

While mental health institutions may implicitly associate the enactment of Tribal identity with risk (i.e., via inclusion of cultural activities as a tool for intervention-prevention), public advertisement of health and wellness messages also create a symbolic association between Tribal identity and risk. On the Sault Tribe reservation, it is common to see flyers and posters encouraging a healthy diet, avoidance of tobacco and alcohol use, respect for women, breaking the cycle of domestic violence, and similar messages. The imagery and captions included in posters consistently promote three themes:

1. A Native American, often dressed in "traditional garb" (regalia, beaded clothing, feathers, Tribal symbols such as the medicine wheel) and expressing Native American physical features (high cheek bones, dark skin/hair/eyes), and in a "traditional" environment, (woodland or natural setting, ceremonial setting) (See Indian Health Services, also posted at NODCP, NWPAIHB, http://216.243.141.9/epicenter/publications)
2. A message of being "at-risk," or broad, threatening facts connecting Native Americans with health risks (diabetes, drug addiction, suicide, low graduation rates, domestic violence) (Ibid.)
3. A remedial message relating back to "traditional" lifeways ("Go back to your traditions/Awakening the Spirit," "My Mind, Body and Spirit are Sacred" (Indian Health Service, accessed 2017); often enhanced by symbol #1 (traditional garb, natural settings)

Such advertisements echo themes of informal conversation in the Sault Tribe community regarding health, specifically the appearance of harmful societal issues is a direct result of 'getting away from traditions,' a belief that 'returning to traditions' can reverse unhealthy lifestyles and health disparities (suicide rates, diabetes, obesity, addiction, family dysfunction), and specific health disparities are inherent traits within indigenous ethnic groups. The combination of these themes, however, may create a symbolic association between 'being Indian,' 'being at-risk' or 'ill,' and loss of cultural traditions/blaming loss of traditions for sickness, amplifying presumptions of inherent risk or vulnerability to physical or mental conditions as an ethnic-racial trait. Focusing on individuals, as members of an ethnic group, socioeconomic class, supposed academic tier and ability (or inability), however, may shift attention away from the social, historical, and economic conditions contributing to or correlating with suicide and behavioral conditions, placing blame on the individual or marginalized class of individuals (Howard and Millard, 1997).

Pushing the semantic description of prevention highlights the limitation of current forms of prevention, whereby social, economic, ethnohistorical, and political aspects of the surrounding environment that place young people at risk are not addressed and protective factors unique to the Tribal community are not advocated (as mainstream treatment, at least). That is to say, mitigating children's exposure to risk factors does not address the deeper socioeconomic, historical, and structural conditions that may be responsible for high rates of suicide (i.e., socioeconomic status, available economic opportunities, criminal recidivism, identity crises, stigma, and gaps in treatment). The early work of May and Dizmang (1974) on the then-rising topic of American Indian youth suicide still bears relevance:

> Simple explanations and solutions for American Indian suicide and other self-destructive behavior are obviously not possible. Any attempt to deal with self-destruction amongst tribes with a high incidence of suicide, alcoholism and violent death would require efforts to bolster the existing sociocultural system and especially the family. (28)

The realization that 'something has to be done' beyond traditional psychological and public health care approaches, however, does little to explain the inability of mainstream methods to curtail suicide on an ethnic level. A 'lack of research,' often a conclusion of indigenous suicide studies, is a fast-disappearing excuse for less effective prevention measures, as indigenous suicide has been a subject of research for nearly fifty years and represents a growing topic of literature in multiple fields (e.g., transcultural psychiatry, anthropology, sociology, nursing science, epidemiology).

Understanding prevention, by default, requires us to question how society frames prevention—what behaviors-health risks are being prevented? Who is at the center of prevention? What is the ultimate goal of prevention? How does society, including at-risk individuals, respond to, recreate, embody, and perpetuate symbols of risk?

The very act of focusing on the individual as the epicenter of risk serves to ascribe responsibility for suicide, health, and sickness to the individual, while ignoring the underlying social issues contributing to youth suicide (i.e., socioeconomic status, poverty, stigma of mental illness and disorders, the misallocation or misappropriation of funding and resources). In a perverse twist, the utilization of 'Indian identity' (i.e., Indian symbols) and the overt inclusion of culture (i.e., cultural activities) within clinical approaches and as a form of mental health intervention associates Indian culture and identity with risk. With analysis of such associations comes the question, "Do Tribal youth associate themselves with risk?" In the section "Conflicted Identity," administrators described youth as accepting of intergenerational anger—"anger that is not theirs—and colonialism as an overriding explanation of current conditions. "Is it possible that, subjected to intergenerational anger, and symbolic associations of "Indianness" and "risk," Tribal youth accept and perpetuate an "at-risk status"?

> Even an effective campaign that garners public sympathy by portraying the youth of a community in crisis as self-destructive and without hope can indirectly reinforce just that kind of self-stereotyping. When suicide becomes a reference point for public sympathy and community mobilization, then all the ideas and emotions associated with it can, among vulnerable individuals, become a reference point for personal agency (Niezen, 2009b: 143). Under these circumstances, the decision to end one's life can be encouraged by collective ideas and actions.
>
> (Niezen, 2015)

The symbolic violence portion of this work, unfortunately, is limited to the above question. However, symbolic violence may prove to be an underutilized concept within indigenous youth suicide studies that points to larger ideological implications, ideology understood here as a system of ideals, shared or understood by society, that guides an individual's and society's moral attitudes regarding political, economic, social, and even medical processes and interactions. An example of ideology in American culture is capitalism, which espouses (amongst other things), that a person must accumulate resources for him or herself, be able to rely on one's self, to be able to 'pull yourself up by your bootstraps.' While capitalism may be seen as a market-based ideology, capitalism also impacts health care settings in that the overriding belief or idea of 'self-reliance' causes society to look upon the sick person as 'at fault,' and individuals as 'at-risk,' while also placing the onus for healing on the individual rather than society as a whole.

While the individual—in this case indigenous youth—may be subject to the harmful effects of ideology (the child is expected to seek help; it is the child's background and/or culture that places him/her at risk), it is possible that the community most impacted by a health disparity may adopt and perpetuate a harmful ideology. A visual representation of a harmful ideology has been discussed above in terms of the "at-risk identity."

According to Althusser's classic description, however, ideology, in its various forms, is not simply *produced*. The ideology in question must be reproduced in order to continue existing and impacting social interactions within various settings (i.e., health care settings). Reproduction, as a final point in Althusser's argument, is reliant on conditions of reproduction (Althusser, 1970). In the case of indigenous youth suicide, the ideological approach to youth suicide (1) places youth at the center of the prevention model, pushing the onus for treatment onto youth, (2) associates cultural background (via symbols, enactment of culture) with risk and discussions of risk, and (3) ignores wider and interconnected social, political, and economic trends impacting treatment of mental health disparities (i.e., conditions of reproduction), such as poverty, disintegration of the family unit, issues of historical trauma, the complexity of Tribal political structures, impact of Tribal politics on treatment initiatives, and potential impact of lack of sovereignty on the mindset of indigenous youth and the vision that youth have for the future.

Works Cited

Althusser, L. (1970) "Ideology and Ideological State Apparatuses (Notes Towards an Investigation)."*La Pensée*. In *Lenin and Philosophy and Other Essays*. New York: Monthly Review Press, 1971. Translated by B. Brewster, Transcribed by A. Blunden.

Freedenthal, S., and Stiffman, A. (2007) "'They Might Think I Was Crazy': Young American Indians' Reasons for Not Seeking Help When Suicidal." *Journal of Adolescent Research*. 22 (1), 58–77.

Howard, M., and Millard, A. V. (1997) *Hunger and Shame: Child Malnutrition and Poverty on Mount Kilimanjaro*. New York and London: Routledge.

Indian Health Service. "Mind, Body, Spirit are Sacred" Poster. Department of Behavior Health. Accessed 2017. https://www.ihs.gov//dbh/includes/themes/responsive2017/display_objects/documents/sap_women.pdf

Kenyon, D., and Hanson, J. (2012) "Incorporating Traditional Culture Into Positive Youth Development Programs With American Indian/Alaska Native Youth." *Child Development Perspectives*. 6 (3), 272–279.

May, P. and Dizmang, L. (1974) "Suicide and the American Indian." *Psychiatric Annals*. 4 (11), 22–23, 27–28.

Michigan Association for Suicide Prevention (2012) "Suicide Prevention Plan for Michigan Evaluation." Michigan Suicide Prevention Coalition. Accessed

February 10, 2017. http://masponweb.org/docs/State%20Suicide%20Prevention%20Plan%20Evaluation.pdf

Michigan Department of Health and Human Services. "Michigan's Youth Suicide Prevention Program." Accessed February 8, 2017. www.michigan.gov/documents/mdch/Michigan_Youth_Suicide_Prevention Program_493960_7.doc

Niezen, Ronald. (2015). "The Durkheim-Tarde Debate and the Social Study of Aboriginal Youth Suicide." *Transcultural Psychiatry*. 52 (1) 96–114.

"Quickfacts, Income and Poverty" by County. Accessed February 22, 2017. www.census.gov/quickfacts/table/AFN120212/26033

Reed, J. (2017) "Changing the Prevention Paradigm." Suicide Prevention Resource Center, Director's Corner. Accessed February 4, 2017. www.sprc.org/news/changing-prevention-paradigm

Sault Tribe, Grant Application. "Sault Tribe Alive Youth (STAY) Project 2008." Grant #1U79SM058400-01. OIA. Accessed August 10, 2014.

Senate Committee on Native American Affairs Hearing. June 25, 2015. "Demanding Results to End Native Youth Suicides."

Walls, M., Hautala, D., and Hurley, J. (2014) "'Rebuilding Our Community': Hearing Silenced Voices on Aboriginal Youth Suicide." *Transcultural Psychiatry*. 51 (1), 47–72.

Twenty feet ahead and to the left, the largest Northern Pike I had ever seen sat hovering on the river bottom, undoubtedly waiting for some prey to swim by. Northern Pike, known for their voracious appetites, feed off of anything from fish not much smaller than themselves, to frogs, rodents, and in the rare instance even ducklings. With its long, predatory jaw and sleek body, Northern Pike strongly resemble its oceangoing cousin the barracuda. And this monster was simply sitting in front of Mathew, as if an offering from the river itself.

Matt hardly needed to say anything. CJ put the boat into a slow drift, turning the paddle to rudder left to give Matt a straight-on shot. Mathew draws the butt of the spear upward at a slant toward the night sky, keeping his right hand high on the back of the ten-foot stave and the left hand down toward the spearhead to guide the coming strike. The barbs dip gently into the water with hardly a ripple, giving the pike no notice of the descending device. At this point, the water plays tricks on the eyes. The spear fisher must know that the spearhead and the fish are not where they seem, but that their images are bent by the water. It takes experience to adjust for this lie in perception.

Six feet from the edge of the boat, the motionless fish is within striking distance. The final moment, the kill shot, is entirely and literally in Mathew's hands. We hold our breath as the boat continues to drift toward the target. Closer . . . closer. Not taking a chance that the giant will sense our presence, Matt does not hesitate, uncoiling his arms and using every bit of the fourteen feet of ash to close the distance between the deadly spearhead and the back of the pike's neck.

Immediately, the river bottom protests the disturbance of its peace by emitting a thick, brown cloud, blinding us to the final verdict. Matt firmly holds the deadly end against the river bottom to keep our quarry in place. When the cloud settles, it is clear that the strike was precise and true. The spear is squarely embedded across the pike's neck, which instantly cut its spinal cord and rendered it lifeless. Other than a few sporadic, reflexive twitches, its spirit is gone.

For several seconds, we take in the moment. 'Holee,' I think to myself, 'that's a big fish.' But we do not wait too long, as Matt begins the second most important phase in the spearing process—bringing the fish successfully into the boat. Even near death a fish can slip off the end of the spear and drag itself into the depths of the river, to die needlessly. To prevent this, Matt points the spear shaft almost straight up, and hand over hand slowly lifts the limp pike out of the water. The barbs, embedded in the other side of the fish, will hold it. In the event the pike begins to slip off, Matt can quickly jam it back into the river bottom until another attempt can be made.

But Matt successfully brings the pike up and over the boat railing and I help ease it off the end of the spear. We sit down and take a longer moment to rest. "That's gotta be the biggest fish you ever caught, spearing or otherwise, huh?" I ask.

"I think so," says Matt, lighting a cigarette.

"Dang Matty, that was a pretty brave shot," Says CJ.

"Well I didn't want to take a chance that it would spook!"

We all sit in the boat, taking glances at the monster lying in the half inch of river water on the bottom of the boat. No gloating. No obnoxious high fives. No 'whoo'-ing. Adrenaline, for sure, courses through Matt's veins, and we each share in the feeling. As in the deer hunt, we exchange jokes and muttered comments on the event, but whenever our eyes shift to the pike it is with a sense of belonging. It was meant to be with us, and though it is exciting to welcome it into our lives at the tip of a spear, it feels natural and normal. As if greeting a friend. It's a sensation that we see in others and feel in ourselves after taking a deer. The hunter anticipates, longs for, but when the game is in his possession, it is as if the moment is shared between the hunter and the animal. In the moments leading to the pull of the trigger, or release of an arrow, the hunter establishes a relationship with the animal. When the deer is in the hunter's possession, it is given an identity by the hunter through his memory of the animal, and the recognition of the personality and character of the deer. The length and growth of the tines, the age, the mannerisms before the shot was taken. Even during cleaning, a careful inspection is often made of the bowels and organs. What did it eat? Was it eating well? Was it sick in any way? And from all of these observations, a biography can be made for the hunter to contemplate. And while we often forgot the ritual, we place tobacco, sometimes rolled out of the end of a full cigarette at the spot that the animal fell or the fish taken as a show of respect—leaving something of value where another thing of value was taken.

Invigorated by this catch, we continue eastward for another few rotations. But our fortune has run thin, and we are well over a mile east of our landing. It is evident that Matt stands the victor on this outing. The sun shows promise of reclaiming the sky from its nocturnal counterpart, so we turn about and begin the arduous journey back. Taking turns between rowing and pushing Huckleberry Finn–style down the river, the exhaustion from nearly eight hours on the river begins to show. Due to our poor coordination with the oars, the boat zig-zags left to right. No matter what we try, we can't seem to keep in a straight line. We don't even have enough energy to properly gripe at each other, though not for lack of anger at the futility of our efforts.

Finally, with perspiration and frustration flowing freely, I loudly and sarcastically say to myself, "Come out to spear, he says. We'll have a great time, he says! Hardly any effort, he says!"

At this zinger we throw our heads back, having to put the paddles down to get the laughter out. Matt declares a smoke break, but CJ decides to continue giving mediocre thrusts with the spear to keep us going. A set of waves from a 1500-foot-long cargo ship, chugging down the center of the canal, rocks the boat. For the second time since we started the excursion, deep purples, reds, and pinks radiate in the sky and reflect off of the water.

"I can't believe Grandma used to walk across this river in the winter time," I say, breaking the silence.

"There was no border back then, huh?" Says CJ. "At least not one that anyone cared about."

"Uncle Mike said she would walk across to visit her grandma," I say.

"Yeah, I guess we were really from Garden River, or at least some of the Mastaw's were," says CJ, alluding to our grandmother's maiden name and the area where many Ojibwa on the American side lived from time to time and had, or I suppose still do have, relatives.

"Uncle Mike said she spoke the language and everything before the Catholic School," I say.

"Probably beat it out of her, I bet," Say's CJ.

Matt continues to take drags on his cigarette. He is usually quiet when CJ, I, or someone else brings up our family history. I don't think it's because he isn't listening or curious. Or proud of our history. I guess the difference between us might be that I want to know and talk about it, whereas he might just want to hear about it and let it be. I don't know.

"Yeah, I think they did. Her brother, our great uncle, even ran off not long after being in the boarding school as a teenager."

"He gave 'em the old, 'thank you, no thank you,'" says CJ.

"Yep. He beat feet," I reply. "But Grandma stayed through it all. Then again, things were probably so poor at home that I guess it didn't hurt to have a kid at a boarding school or at a brother or sister's house for a while."

A breeze ripples the surface of the colorful water, gently waking the Saint Marys River from its dreams of ghosts floating on its surface, chasing fish in the night by lantern-light. The wind provides some relief to the passengers of the tiny boat as well. I strip off my sweater before we take to the oars again. Sweat and laughter flowing freely from our bodies, we row the flat bottom boat back to Uncle Mike's landing.

There are no peoples however primitive without religion and magic. Nor are there, it must be added at once, any [indigenous peoples] lacking either in the scientific attitude or in science, though this lack has been frequently attributed to them. In every primitive community, studied by trustworthy and competent observers, there have been found two clearly distinguishable domains, the Sacred and the Profane; in other words, the domain of Magic and Religion and that of Science . . . One achievement of modern anthropology we shall not question: the recognition that magic and religion are not merely a doctrine or a philosophy, not merely an intellectual body of opinion, but a special mode of behavior, a pragmatic attitude built up of reason, feeling, and will alike. It is a mode of action as well as a system of belief, and a sociological phenomenon as well as a personal experience. But with all this, the exact relation between the social and the individual contributions to religion is not clear, as we have seen from the exaggerations committed on either side. Nor is it clear what are the respective shares of emotion and reason. All these questions will have to be dealt with by future anthropology.

Malinowski, *Magic, Science and Religion: And Other Essays* (1954: 17)

6 Conclusion

Meanings . . .

Extensive quotes, anecdotes, excerpts of field notes and transcripts, and creative ethnographic writing display the lived realities of the Bowheting Ojibwa as they respond to youth suicide and mental health disparity. Reflecting on stigma, reporting procedures, historical trauma, and other interrelated aspects of youth suicide, this community's experiences closely resemble the national picture of indigenous youth suicide. Oral traditions and histories of the Anishnaabek provide an entry point to read attitudes toward life, death, health, treatment, and youth suicide, and construct treatment models relevant to cultural realities. Brother John, for example, discusses suicide and health in terms consistent with a wellness paradigm, speaking of health in a "good way," as opposed to health and individuals as a subject of negativity (risk). Brother John and several interviewees (traditional healers, mental health administrator) also emphasize the impact of politics, economy, community, and extended family on suicide (impact of casino industry and gambling addiction, lack of monetary support for youth programming, criminal recidivism), which focuses efforts outward, toward the institutions and ideologies that surround youth, rather than inward toward youth. The holistic orientation toward health and wellbeing is supported by the very definition of suicide—"one who is not loved"—which implies that true death is not considered a loss of biological life, but of social life.

Rather than concentrate on statistical analysis of risk and protective factors, this work is an attempt at mixed-methods research, sketching an ethnohistorical portrait of youth suicide as a behavioral phenomenon that crosses social, historical, and cultural lines. The emphasis on wider historical forces influencing youth suicide follows on the heels of recent mixed-methods approaches utilizing qualitative methods, ethnographic information, and collaboration with, rather than career use of, indigenous peoples. Collaborating with indigenous communities creates a central space for emic or insider theories on youth suicide that emanate from the culture of the community, pushes the bounds of future research, and validates indigenous viewpoints on the origins and perpetuation of health disparities (Walls, Hautala, and Hurley, 2014: Discussion; see Briggs, 2004).

Shifting from risk factors to potential barriers to treatment, relief and suicide prevention-intervention exposes roadblocks that exist within the medical-mental health care system and the community at large—poverty, stigma, and symbolic violence. Symbols associating indigeneity with risk may create, reinforce, and perpetuate stereotypes of Indians as at risk for health disparities, thereby pressuring a sub-set of the indigenous population to internalize risk as a component of Indian identity or "Indianness." In other words, for some Tribal members, living the "Rez-life" and being a real 'NDN' means accepting risk factors, as well as certain protective factors, as a status quo—normalizing substance abuse, dysfunctional family structure, and other risk factors contributing to suicide and poor health. In this scenario, identity, rather than becoming a protective factor, becomes a barrier to escaping harmful life circumstances (see Dressler and Bindon, 2000, for examples of similar influence of cultural consonance on health in African American communities).

The semantic exploration of prevention leads to a more critical interpretation of how we treat illness and health disparities and presents the argument that current research and treatment approaches leave out the social and historical determinants of health. Explanations for current prevention-intervention models almost inevitably or at least in this case loop back to the impact of ideological components of the treatment process.

Oral histories and traditions, as well as anecdotes, personal stories, poetry—described as the creative writing component—are present throughout this work. Stories of Nanabozhoo Epighizhmuk, the Weendigo, and countless other myths provide more than simple entertainment. Such stories provide a moral instruction and an approach toward observing and understanding human behavior: The conflict between Nanabozhoo and Epighizhmuk brings to light reconciliation with the past, which in this work takes the form of intergenerational anger and historical trauma. The Weendigo provides a stark reminder of the dark power of greed on the part of pharmaceuticals as a component of a larger medical-industrial complex that sees humans primarily as consumers. Expanded in political and economic scope and complexity, Tribal enterprise and government may fail to connect and respond to the lived realities of Tribal members, seen by one administrator as "the cost of civilization."

Ceremonial processes and funeral traditions treat death as a "world changing" or "walking on," a period of transition within a continuous process of life. Treating the deceased as a living entity allows the memory of the deceased, as it exists for individuals and the community, to proceed in a spiritual life cycle, as opposed to holding the memory of a person to the place and time of death—a memory that "stops at 16." Ojibwa view the transitory nature of the spirit as continuing according to stages of life and traveling beyond the funeral and memorialization process. Including these views, gained in traditional education, in discussions of life, death, and suicide may nullify false or exaggerated expressions of connectedness to the deceased, and other, more dangerous ways of connecting with the dead enacted through suicide pacts, imitation, or clusters.

From oral histories and traditions to select anecdotes gained from observation, the stories shared in this work provide examples of underlying factors for suicide ideation and culturally based approaches to remedying conditions while avoiding the perpetuation of 'at-risk identity.' Including creative writing and excerpts from transcripts and field notes allows the reader to share the ethnographic lens and, more specifically, the investigation of cultural concepts and practices—identity, risk, prevention, health, and death—that are the basis for this study. The writing style allows the invested lay audience to participate in the process of analysis of key observations, regardless of any agreement with the researcher's interpretation. The writing style, then, facilitates collaboration on the broadest levels possible by building on the expectation, rather than a simple invitation, of further analysis and dialogue within a wider audience of academics, policymakers, and invested lay people.

Researchers, lawmakers, and indigenous communities speaking on youth suicide often include, within the conclusion, recommendations that American and Canadian governments provide additional resources to Tribal communities, advertising the treaty obligations and lack of funding for research and treatment (e.g., Dorgan, 2010). This study does not refute the call for increased resources, and supports through evidence the need for resources (see Barriers, e.g., "no psychiatrists," and need for inpatient services). Insisting that the primary cause of health disparities amongst Tribal communities revolves around historical trauma, colonization, and lack of resources, however, unwittingly depicts Tribes as dependent states. In a general sense, viewing and treating Tribes as victims erases Tribal agency, and more specifically, discounts the possibility that Tribal society may independently engage in structural and symbolic violence, contributing to underlying conditions for youth suicide. Discounting Tribal agency is a common theme in indigenous youth suicide literature, which as far as I am aware is a novel and contentious statement. Regardless, it is a statement that the academic community has a responsibility to address. Continuing to depend on Western governments for resources and aid while blaming previous and current issues on Western government and society (as warranted as it may be) may push Tribes away from available cultural resources and an attitude of self-determination, and closer to a historically paternal relationship. The resulting erosion of ethnic agency amongst current and future generations of indigenous youth is an example of when 'speaking to power' becomes 'the speech of the powerless.'

The subtitle to this work, "The Meanings of Life, Death, and Youth Suicide," implies that youth suicide presents multiple, perhaps interconnected, meanings—Meanings of life and death; Meanings that communities, that fathers, mothers, siblings, grandparents, aunts, uncles, cousins, and friends attribute to tragic loss; Meanings of treatment, prevention, and medicine; that Value-Meanings of research—not simply the what and how that results from data, methodologies, and theories, but the why that results from cultural values; Meanings of youth suicide as an event embodying the larger cultural history of the Anishnaabek; Meanings of the community's responses to youth suicide and mental health disparity as an enactment of a vision of the future for an entire people.

The main title of this work, *Guided by the Spirits*, introduces an Anishnaabek view of human behavior—past, present, and future—as holistic, interconnected, and guided by unseen forces felt and experienced on a daily basis. Malinowski discovered, when contemplating the "Sacred and the Profane," or the realms of "Magic and Religion, and that of Science," that "magic and religion"

> are not merely a doctrine or a philosophy, not merely an intellectual body of opinion, but a special mode of behavior, a pragmatic attitude built up of reason, feeling, and will alike. It is a mode of action as well as a system of belief, and a sociological phenomenon as well as a personal experience (Malinowski, 1954: 17).

The complete title outlines the goal of this work, which is to question the meanings of a behavior that we construct, the path that we take to gain knowledge about that behavior, and why we observe, interpret, and construct meanings. With that said, I leave it to my community and to the reader to make meaning of youth suicide in an Ojibwa community.

Works Cited

Briggs, C. (2004) "Theorizing Modernity Conspiratorially: Science, Scale, and the Political Economy of Public Discourse in Explanations of a Cholera Epidemic." *American Ethnologist*. 31 (2), 164–187.

Dressler, W., and Bindon, J. (2000) "The Health Consequences of Cultural Consonance: Cultural Dimensions of Lifestyle, Social Support and Arterial Blood Pressure in an African American Community." *American Anthropologist*. 102 (2), 244–260.

Dorgan, B. (2010) "The Tragedy of Native American Youth Suicide." *Psychological Services* 7 (3) 213 –218.

Malinowski, B. (1954). *Magic, science and religion: And other essays / With an introd. by Robert Redfield*. (Garden City, New York; Doubleday anchor books).

Walls, M., Hautala, D., and Hurley, J. (2014) "'Rebuilding Our Community': Hearing Silenced Voices on Aboriginal Youth Suicide." *Transcultural Psychiatry*. 51 (1), 47–72.

Epilogue

I remember playing on the rocks outside my uncle's home on the banks of the Saint Marys River with my brothers, sister, cousins—we all remember those days in the sun, running sprints on the tops of great boulders left by glaciers thousands of years ago. My father and uncles taught me to spear pike, sucker, perch, and bass out of the river at night. In the day, we went on expeditions, picking blueberries, raspberries, and blackberries. The delicious jams and pies my grandmother and Aunt Nancy concocted were always worth the annoying sting of the raspberry vine, and aching back that came from bending down to the blueberry bush—which always devolved from bending, to kneeling, and ta heck with it—eating the precious collection of berries, lying down and perhaps falling asleep under a clear blue sky. We tested our nerve by swimming in the ice-cold waters, using pieces of driftwood as makeshift vessels to reach and explore the small islands that lay off shore. And if we had not swum out to those islands in the day, we could always wait until dark and let the voracious mosquitos carry us over the water.

Such picturesque moments on the island are not the only memories in my mind, but they are the ones that I cling to and keep closest to my heart. Even now, I can hear the water lapping against the dock and shore, the loon crying, and the gentle sound of wind rustling leaves of the birch trees that sprout along the shoreline and reach out, as if trying to grasp a distant relative across the water. I hope to bring my son to that place, to give him such memories. I want him to cross the Straits of Mackinac and feel what I felt. That I am in my homeland. That the air, the ground under my feet, the people, the sun all feel somehow natural and good, as if this is the place I am meant to be. When my wife speaks of Puerto Rico, she speaks with the same conviction, and that is a feeling we share. My blood is tied to Bowheting.

Now I am older and I have a family. I began to understand what it is to be Ojibwa from my teachers at the sweat lodge and in preparation for a fast when I was younger. More importantly, I learn what it is to be

Ojibwa through being a father and a husband—not from what a card says about my blood quantum or a political recognition.

Now I run on different rocks and swim in different currents—exploring islands made of memory and history, tradition and belief, culture and identity—gathering stories of people's lives. Throughout the explorations and gathering of stories, I cannot help but wonder—what is our story? What has it become? This study centered, whether by design or happenstance, on identity, yet the question of who we are as a people is elusive. What is it to be Ojibwa?

Sometimes I think we forgot who we are, or more specifically, where we came from. Explorers, we traveled tens of thousands of miles across ocean, forest, mountain, and river, along the way adapting to new climates and ecosystems, creating technologies, building structures, and learning the value of new plants and herbs as foods and medicines. Looking at the health disparities and social issues that face us, we can search for fault in a history of colonization and settlement—or we can de-colonize, disconnecting ourselves from an imagined harness, a fated subjection to painful circumstance. Many individuals, families, and in some ways our ethnicity is caught in a cycle of distress, intergenerational anger, political dependency, and conflicted identity. While I hint at that belief in the above writing, I express it openly here. Only we have the power to perpetuate, or if we choose, break this cycle that is defined by not only youth suicide, but diabetes, commercial tobacco addiction, cancer, and many other health disparities that are connected with larger social and historical determinants of health.

Our lives can be chained to our fears and reservations, as we continue to engage in the casino industry and pursue false profits—or we can step out of the comfortable harness of dependency. Each step toward a hopeful future is a confrontation with our inner fears—fear of stepping down a path from the hopeless and known to the hopeful and unknown. With each step forward or backward, we shape our story as individuals, families, communities, and as a people. As explorers, and receivers of prophecy, the Spirits guided us. Perhaps, if we listen, we can be Guided by the Spirits again.

Children run through the green grass at the bottom of the valley, laughing and jumping in the warm rays of the evening sun.

It is that special time, just before night descends. It is a time when, much like the morning, the world is in transition, and prayer and ceremony are especially powerful. The almost blinding reds and oranges stab through the pine, oak, cedar, and brush, causing shadow and light to undulate as the wind sways the forest. The sun wraps around the children, irradiating their skin. The wind whips long hair in and out of their eyes.

Their laughter, like the breeze, drifts across my ears. I sit on a grassy hill above the valley, with its orchard of fruit trees, each hanging heavy with fruit—an easy harvest.

The scent of Sweetgrass, Mother's Hair, floats on the wind.

I wake, slowly pulling away from this other world—a world of Spirits.

Appendix
Interview Questions

(Asterisks denote questions altered from original wording or added in the course of fieldwork. The language of the questions is copied directly from the interview question sheet.)

Professional responsibilities, place in organization

What position do you hold and how long have you held it?
Have you ever held any other positions which related to Tribal youth or the areas of public health?*
How would you describe the responsibilities of your position?
What motivates you to complete your responsibilities?
How do your responsibilities relate to Tribal youth?

Youth suicide, general

(Discuss the definition of "youth" as included in this study.)
Is youth suicide a significant issue in the Sault Tribe community?
When did youth suicide become a significant issue in the Sault Tribe community?
Why did youth suicide become a significant issue in the Sault Tribe community?
How would you describe those who are most at risk for attempting or completing suicide in the Sault Tribe community?
What are the risk factors for youth suicide in the Sault Tribe community?

Ideas of life, death, and suicide

What is death?*
How do people in the Sault Tribe community treat death, or react to death—as families, individuals, and as a community (spiritually, emotionally, socially)?

How do youth respond to death?*
What happens when a person dies? (To the person; and later within the community)*
Is there a "good" death? A "bad" death? A timely death or untimely death?*
What is suicide?
Are there good reasons for suicide, or reasons that are socially acceptable?
Is suicide seen as an acceptable death or an unacceptable death?
How would a person be remembered or thought of after a completed suicide?
Does the acceptability or unacceptability of suicide affect how a person who completed suicide is remembered?
How is the family remembered/treated?*
How has the Sault Tribe community responded to youth suicide as an issue?
Do you know how the community responds, or has responded, to attempted suicide? A completed suicide?
What is life?*
What is a good life? A bad life?*
How is a good life attained?*
What does youth suicide mean for Tribal society? (Historically/culturally)

Mental health care/traditional health care, stigma and suicide

How do Tribal youth address their personal, emotional, or mental health issues?
How often do Tribal members who have significant personal, emotional, or mental issues (depression, anger issues, behavioral disorders) seek help or assistance with such issues?
What are some barriers for mental health assistance? For youth?
Why would a Tribal youth NOT seek mental health assistance?
Are Tribal members who have significant personal, emotional, or mental issues treated differently in the community? (Depression, anger issues, behavioral disorders) If yes, how so?
Do Tribal members, especially youth, avoid or not seek mental health care due to how the community views those who have mental health issues?
What are common treatments for mental health issues in the Tribal community? For youth?*
What is "Traditional" medicine?

How often do Tribal members seek "traditional medicine" for personal, emotional, or mental issues?

Are there barriers for those seeking traditional medicine? For youth?

When experiencing mental or emotional discomfort/pain, what are the sources of "help" or relief commonly sought by youth? How do they seek out these sources?*

Is race a source of stigma for Tribal members? In or out of the Tribal community?*

How do Tribal people display their identity in daily life?*

Do Tribal members change or alter their identity and how they display identity, according to the people they are near or the places they happen to be?*

Administrative and community responses to suicide, general

(Note on what is meant by "administration")

How has the Tribal administration responded to youth suicide?

How has the mental health community responded to youth suicide?

How has the educational community responded to youth suicide?

Do you have a historical or cultural department that can provide advice or guidance on public health issues, as those issues may be affected by historical or cultural factors?

How have historical or cultural departments responded to youth suicide?

Have traditional healers been involved in addressing youth suicide?*

How has the Sault Tribe Board of Directors or the Chairman's office responded to youth suicide?

How has the academic community been involved in addressing youth suicide in the community?

What are the resources for youth suicide prevention activities and programs?*

How are those resources sought out/gained?*

Prevention, intervention, resilience, and suicide

What is suicide prevention?

What could prevent youth from turning to suicide as an option?

What is suicide intervention?

How would you describe the context and process of intervention, as you are concerned with the intervention process? (Example)

Is there a reporting and treatment process for suicidal individuals or those with serious mental health issues? If so, please describe it.*

What is your involvement with youth suicide prevention or intervention efforts?
How can we understand youth suicide? How can youth suicide be studied in a way that facilitates prevention?
What is resilience?
How do you think youth can become resilient to youth suicide or issues which contribute to youth suicide?

The social sciences and youth suicide prevention, prevention studies

(Interviewer: Note what is meant by "social sciences")
How has youth suicide been studied in the community? (Via administration, social sciences, or the mental health community)
What is your experience with social scientists or social science studies of youth suicide or related behavioral issues in the Sault Tribe community?
What is, or has been, your involvement with critical studies of youth suicide?
What are your feelings toward me as a social scientist and this project's approach to youth suicide and youth suicide prevention?*
Do you have any resources that you would like to share with this project? (Data, publications, suggestions for sources of information)*

Additional Sources

2009 Senate Bill 1014: Create Native American language teacher certification exception. State of Michigan. Accessed August 26, 2014. www.michiganvotes.org/2009-SB-1014

Benton-Banai, Edward. (1988) *The Mishomis Book: The Voice of the Ojibway*. Saint Paul, Minnesota: Red School House.

Brazao, Dale. "Months Later, Teen Suicides Still Plague Reserve 47 Attempts made since Aid Promised." *Toronto Star*: 0. Aug 09 1994. Accessed November 8, 2013. http://search.proquest.com/docview/437070241?pq-origsite=summon

Brown, P. (1952) "Changes in Ojibwa social control." *American Anthropologist*. 54 (1) 57–70.

Bruckert, Chris, Hannem, Stacey. (2012) *Stigma revisited: Implications of the mark*. Ottawa: University of Ottawa Press.

Chan, K.P.M. (2001) "Suicide in response to changing societies." *Child and Adolescent Psychiatric Clinics of North America*. 10 (4) 777–795.

Christakis, N. and Fowler, J. (2013) "Social Contagion Theory: Examining Dynamic Social Relationships and Human Behavior." *Statistics in Medicine*. 32 (4) 556–577.

Clark, T., Robinson, E., Crengle, S., Fleming, T., Ameratunga, S., Simon, D., Bearinger, L., Sieving, R., Saewyc, E. (2011) "Risk and Protective Factors for Suicide Attempt Among Indigenous Maori Youth in New Zealand: The Role of Family Connection." *Journal of Aboriginal Health*, March, 2011. National Aboriginal Health Organization (NAHO).

Clifford, James. (2004) "Looking Several Ways: Anthropology and Native Heritage in Alaska." *Current Anthropology*. 45 (1) 5–30.

Coupe, Nikki. (2000) Maori Suicide Rate Under Investigation. *The Press*, October 12, 2000: 9.

Cwik, M., Barlow, A., Goklish, N., Larzelere-Hinton, F., Tingy, L. (2012) "Community Based Surveillance and Case Management for Suicide Prevention: An American Indian Tribally Initiated System." *American Journal of Public Health*. 104 (3) 18–23.

Goodkind, Gorman, Hess, Parker & Hough (2015). Reconsidering Culturally Competent Approaches to American Indian Healing and Well-Being, *Qualitative Health Research*. 25 (4) 486–499

Hallowell, A., Brown, J., and Gray, S. (2010). *Contributions to Ojibwe studies: Essays, 1934–1972* / A. Irving Hallowell; edited and with introductions by Jennifer S. H. Brown and Susan Elaine Gray. (Critical studies in the history of anthropology); Lincoln; University of Nebraska Press.

Hummingbird, L. (2011) "The Public Health Crisis of Native American Youth Suicide." *NASN School Nurse.*

Jackson, D. (2010) "Shelter in place: a First Nation community in Canada's Chemical Valley" *Interdisciplinary Environmental Review*, 11 (4) 249–262

Jackson, D. (2011) "Scents of Place: The Displacement of a First Nations Community in Canada." *American Anthropologists.* 113 (4) 606–618

Johnston, Basil. (1995) *The Manitous: The Spiritual World of the Ojibwa.* HarperCollins; New York.

Kenyon, D., Hanson, J. (2012) "Incorporating Traditional Culture into Positive Youth Development Programs with American Indian/Alaska Native Youth." *Child Development Perspectives.* 6 (3) 272–279.

Kovacs, M., Beck, A., and Weissman, A. (1975). "Hopelessness." *Suicide and Life-Threatening Behavior.* 5 (2) 98–103.

Kral, Michael J. (2012) "Postcolonial Suicide Among Inuit in Arctic Canada." *Culture, Medicine, and Psychiatry.* 36 (2) 306–325.

Kristen, Jacklin. (2009) "Diversity within: Deconstructing Aboriginal community health in Wikwemikong Unceded Indian Reserve." *Social Science & Medicine.* 68 (5) 980–989.

Lassiter, Eric. (2005) "Collaborative Ethnography and Public Anthropology." *Current Anthropology.* 46 (1) 83–106.

Landes, Ruth. (1969) *Ojibwa Sociology.* New York: AMS Press.

Le, T.N. and Gobert, J.M. (2015) "Translating and Implementing a Mindfulness-Based Youth Suicide Prevention Intervention in a Native American Community." *Journal of Child and Family Studies.* 24 (1) 12–23

McIntosh, John L., & Santos, John F. (1980). "Suicide among Native Americans: A Compilation of Findings." *Omega: Journal of Death and Dying*, 11(4) 303–316.

Russell J. Barber and Frances F. Berdan, "The Scope of Ethnohistory," *The Emperor's Mirror: Understanding Cultures through Primary Sources* (Tucson: University of Arizona Press, 1998), 5–32.

Sarche, M. C., Spicer, P., Farrell, P., & Fitzgerald, H. E. (Eds.). (2011). *American Indian and Alaskan Native children and mental health: Development, context, prevention, and treatment.* Santa Barbara, CA: ABC-CLIO, LLC.

Smith, D. (2008) "Finding Hope for the Innocent Ones." *Toronto Star.*

Spaulding, John M. (1985) "Recent Suicide Rates Among Ten Ojibwa Indian Bands in Northwestern Ontario." *OMEGA—Journal of Death and Dying.* 16 (4) 347–354.

Suicide Prevention Resource Center. (2013). "Suicide among racial/ethnic populations in the U.S.: American Indians/Alaska Natives." Waltham, MA: Education Development Center, Inc. (Funded by U.S. Department of Health and Human Service's Substance Abuse and Mental Health Services Administration. Accessed November, 2016. http://www.sprc.org/sites/sprc.org/files/library/AI_AN%20Sheet%20Aug%2028 %202013%20Final.pdf

Trouillot, Michel-Rolph. (1997) *Silencing the Past: Power and Production of History*. Beacon Press; Boston.

Walls, M. L., Gonzalez, J. Galdney, T. & Onello, E. (2015). Unconscious bias. Racial microagressions in American Indian Health Care. Journal of American Board of Family Medicine, 28 (2) 231–239.

Warhol, Larisa. "Native American Language Policy in the United States." *Heritage Briefs*. Center for Applied Linguistics, 2011. Accessed August 26, 2014. www.cal.org/heritage/pdfs/briefs/native-american-language-policy.pdf

Warren, William. (1885) *History of the Ojibway People*. Minnesota Historical Society.

Zizek, Slavoj. (2008) *Violence: Six Sideways Reflections (Big Ideas/Small Books)*. Picador.

Index

www.ingramcontent.com/pod-product-compliance
Ingram Content Group UK Ltd.
Pitfield, Milton Keynes, MK11 3LW, UK
UKHW021959180926
475701UK00003B/98